4 -05

D1556126

WITHDRAWN

13

GROWING UP IN THE
PLAYGROUND

Social Worlds of Childhood

General Editor: Rom Harré

Growing up in the Playground

The Social Development of Children

Andy Sluckin

ROUTLEDGE & KEGAN PAUL
LONDON, BOSTON AND HENLEY

First published in 1981
by Routledge & Kegan Paul Ltd
39 Store Street,
London WC1E 7DD,
9 Park Street,
Boston, Mass. 02108, USA and
Broadway House,
Newtown Road,
Henley-on-Thames,
Oxon RG9 1EN
Printed in Great Britain by
Billing & Sons Ltd
Guildford, Surrey

British Library Cataloguing in Publication Data

Sluckin, Andy
Growing up in the playground. - (Social worlds
of childhood)
1. Child development   2. Socialization
3. Play
I. Title   II. Series
305.2'3   HQ783

ISBN 0 7100 0788 4

Contents

General Editor's Preface

For most of us childhood is a forgotten and even a rejected time.
The aim of this series is to recover the flavour of childhood and
adolescence in a systematic and sympathetic way. The frame of
mind cultivated by the authors as investigators is that of anthropologists who glimpse a strange tribe across a space of forest
and millennia of time. The huddled group on the other side of
the school playground and the thumping of feet in the upstairs
rooms mark the presence of a strange tribe. This frame of mind
is deliberately different from that of the classical investigators
of child psychology, who have brought adult concepts to bear
upon the understanding of children's thoughts and actions, and
have looked at childhood primarily as a passage towards the skills
and accomplishments and distortions of adults. In these studies
the authors try to look upon the activities of children as
autonomous and complete in themselves. Of course, not all the
activities of childhood could be treated in this way. Rather than
being in opposition to the traditional kind of study, the work
upon which this series is based aims to amplify our understanding by bringing to light aspects of childhood which usually
remain invisible when it is looked at in the traditional way. The
ethogenic method is in use throughout the studies represented
in this series, that is the children themselves are the prime
sources of theories about their actions and thoughts and of
explanations of the inwardness of their otherwise mysterious
activities.

Acknowledgments

The material for this book comes mainly from conversations that
I 'overheard' in the playgrounds of two Oxford schools. Few of
the children realized that what they said would be 'taken down
and used in evidence', though not I hope 'against them'. Indeed,
my excuse for prying at all is a belief that the insights to be
gained in this way into an otherwise hidden aspect of children's
lives can only lead to an added respect for them. In order to
protect the participants' privacy, however, I have given each
one of them, both adults and children, a pseudonym.

The research reported in this book was first undertaken as
a doctoral thesis, 'Experience in the playground and the
development of competence' and presented to the University of
Oxford in 1980. In preparing a version that teachers, parents
and all those interested in children can easily understand and,
I hope, enjoy, I have considerably simplified much of the text.
In so doing, the work has gained in clarity, for I have followed
the principle that all important ideas should be capable of
simple expression. Any material from the thesis that failed this
test was discarded. Students wishing to follow up any of the
ideas, or embark upon their own study of children's lives 'as
they are really lived', are referred to the Notes and Bibliography
at the end of the text.

During the past five years I have received financial support
from The Social Science Research Council, London, first in
Oxford and latterly in Edinburgh. I am grateful to them, as I
am to friends and family who have made invaluable comments
on the manuscript. I particularly wish to thank Peter Smith,
Margaret Manning and Rom Harré. I have learned much from
them, although the original idea that what children do at playtime might be worth studying came from Peter Bryant. Publication is with permission of the Oxfordshire Education Authority
and the Head Teachers of the schools involved. I also acknowledge
the Hogarth Press for permission to quote from 'Cider with Rosie'
by Laurie Lee.

1

'What do you think playtime's for?'

Author: What do you think playtime's for?
Jon (5 years): I think it's to make me grow up a bit.
Author: How?
Jon: Well, I think running around and playing hopscotch and
     lying down make me grow up a bit. Well, I mean I get a
     bit more excited in the playground.
Author: You say it helps you to grow up?
Jon: No that doesn't mean anything. I can't think of anything
     else what it's for.
Author: What about playing hopscotch, do you think it's a
     very grown-up thing to do?
Jon: No, of course not.
Author: I thought you said playing hopscotch makes you grow
     up?
Jon: It doesn't make you grow up right to the ceiling!
Author: What does it do?
Jon: It makes me grow up extremely slowly.

The developing child comes under many influences. The first
is that of the parents, but children do not stay forever within
the confines of the home. By the time they are five or six, they
start to spend much of their day at school. Some children have
a difficult settling-in period, but others take to it like a duck
to water. If the classroom is often strange and frightening to a
young child, the break between lessons can be worse. For in
the playground there are even more children confined together.
We all know that there are opportunities to learn at home and
in the classroom, but is there anything to be learnt at playtime?
This book is about my attempt to find out.

When I asked the teachers and children at an Oxford First
School, 'What do you think playtime's for?', both groups gave
similar replies. 'It's a time when they can let off steam', 'the
teachers get a break', 'we get fresh air and exercise'. 'But are
the children learning anything?', I insisted. The adults
elaborated upon five-year-old Jon's suggestion that 'playtime
makes me grow up extremely slowly.' 'They learn how to get on
with one another and make friends', 'to sink their own selfish
interests from time to time in order to become part of a game',
and 'to cope with each other as people, as human beings with
equal rights. They need to give and take equally with nobody
interfering.'

Few of these teachers, however, had a clear idea of just what

their pupils do when they are by themselves. It's a world that
may seem more or less closed to adults, but this is mainly
because we choose to ignore it. Most of the teachers explained
that they abhor playground duty and only really take note of
what is going on around them should a problem arise. It is no
coincidence that Head Teachers avoid this chore. Likewise,
parents rush past the playground so as to get away from the
deafening din of their offspring who scream at the tops of their
voices. But is it all just running about with no particular pur-
pose other than to let off steam?

Iona and Peter Opie, lifelong collectors of children's folklore,
have looked more closely at just what goes on at playtime and
they reveal a far more complex world and one that is immensely
rich in tradition. The material for their books 'The Lore and
Language of Schoolchildren' and 'Children's Games in Street
and Playground' was collected during the 1950s and 1960s. They
describe the seasonal customs, initiation rites, superstitious
practices and beliefs, rhymes and chants, catcalls and retorts,
stock jokes, ruderies, riddles, slang epithets, nicknames and
innumerable traditional games common in playgrounds throughout the British Isles. But although their findings have become
widely known, the teachers and parents that I have met have
been sceptical that this world extended into their own back
yard. Though they fondly recollect the traditions of their own
schooldays, they lament that the impact of television and other
aspects of modern culture have done much to destroy the
continuity of oral lore. But in two Oxford schools at least, I
can report that the playground world lives on.

You don't have to look that closely to realize that children
at playtime are not 'just like little savages', but there may still
be a sense in which playground life can be said to be primitive.
Is this where the social skills necessary for adult life are
learnt? Is this where children begin to master how to manipulate
their peers with words alone? At times children's sophisticated
use of language is strikingly similar to that of adults. According
to the Opies, the day to day running of playground life involves
'affidavits, promissory notes, claims, deeds of conveyance,
receipts and notices of resignation, all of which are verbal and
all sealed by the utterance of ancient words which are recognized and considered binding by the whole community.' There
are certainly parallels between the methods of management
of the child and adult social worlds, but just how important is
experience in the playground? To find out I decided to make
my own observations of the social interactions of five- to ten-
year-olds at playtime.

HOW TO WATCH CHILDREN

The study of learning, or rather the impact of experience on
development, has always been a central theme in psychology.

But few researchers have investigated learning in the natural
environment, preferring instead the more controlled but
artificial conditions of the psychological laboratory. Although
such an approach has been dominant, it has never been without
criticism. Many researchers have suggested their own alternative methods. They stress the need for careful and systematic
observation in natural surroundings, and this goes far beyond
the occasional opportunities we all have for looking. Both
zoologists and anthropologists have always done this, but each
in their own characteristic way. The influence of both these
disciplines can be seen in the few observational studies that
have taken place in the playground.

The influence of zoology arises out of the success over the
past thirty years of systematic observation of animals. Why not
try the same method with humans? In just the same way as
zoologists were careful not to interact with, and so influence
the behaviour of, ducks, chickens, monkeys and other crea-
tures, so the psychologists were with human beings. They
became non-participant observers who noted down whenever
any of a long list of carefully defined categories of behaviour
occurred.

Despite the small number of such studies at playtime, those
that have been conducted span many countries and give a clear
indication of much that is easily quantifiable about human
behaviour. One researcher observed three- to eleven-year-olds
in United States, Swiss and Ethiopian playgrounds. Another
made extensive notes on the play of five- to seven-year-olds
in playgrounds in Kyoto (Japan), Delissaville (Australian
Aborigine), Hong Kong (Chinese), Bali, Ceylon, New Delhi,
Pondicherry, Kenya (Kikuyu) and Crown Point in New Mexico
(Navajo). A third, Rivka Eifermann, recorded the play and
games of Israeli children. All three projects provide much basic
data about such features of playground life as the amount of
interaction, the size of sub-groups of children and their sex
and age composition. For instance, some sex segregation was
seen everywhere, though there was least among the Kikuyu and
most in Ceylon, but in all settings boys tended to play with
boys and girls with girls. Similarly, in all cultures it was the
boys who were more aggressive whilst the girls spent more
time in conversation.

Eifermann's observations come nearest of all to our theme of
growing up in the playground. She was able to investigate
whether the way of life of the Israeli kibbutzim reflects itself
in the children's patterns of play. Six- to fourteen-year-olds
were watched for about a year during playtime in two kibbutz
and two moshav schools. The moshav makes a good comparison,
for although these are also rural communities, they differ by
being co-operative settlements in which the families only pool
their incomes to a degree. In contrast, the kibbutz family is
totally subordinated to the community.

The games in the two kinds of school showed clear differences.

'The children of the dream', as Bruno Bettelheim once called
those born in the kibbutz, played games which tended to reflect
the values of co-operation and egalitarianism to a greater
degree than the moshav children. Apparently, it is not that
competition as such is shunned, but rather that its potential
impact is overcome by the children playing games which stress
a good deal of co-operation within sub-groups. Similarly, in
any game with single children competing against each other,
there were rarely any roles that allowed either of the participants an advantage.

How does this choice of activities come about? Perhaps unduly
competitive games are discouraged by adults. Alternatively, it
may be that the children themselves decide between different
kinds of activities, preferring those that conform with what
they see going on around them. Eifermann unfortunately did
not examine this issue, but her findings do support those
theories of play which stress the preparatory and exploratory
character of children's playful activities. She shares in a
tradition that stretches back at least to Plato and Aristotle, who
regarded play as 'tools for young builders', and is echoed
nowadays by Jean Piaget, the grandfather of modern child
psychology. It is perhaps worth adding that Eifermann's results
tend to conflict with theories that have emerged under the
influence of Sigmund Freud, which have a common theme that
children's games express a hidden revolt against adult values.
Indeed, there has never been a lack of theorists willing to
speculate about the functions of play, nor of authors eager
to collect and summarize the disparate and often irreconcilable
viewpoints. Yet paradoxically there has been little straight-
forward description of what children actually do in the
playground.

Whereas those studies influenced by zoology observe people
as if they were just another species, and banish from their
minds any preconceptions they might have about the nature of
human societies, anthropologists have done quite the reverse.
Their method is to go and live amongst the people they want to
study. They learn their language and ways and try to understand the culture from within. At around the same time in the
1920s when the young Margaret Mead went to the South Sea
Polynesian island of Samoa to find out about the lives of girls
and women of the community, the young Jean Piaget was likewise participating in games of marbles with four- to twelve-year-
old boys in and around Geneva. The book that arose from this
study was called 'The Moral Judgment of the Child' in which
Piaget was concerned, as the title says, with moral judgments;
that is, a child's ideas about rules, justice, ethical behaviour
and so on. He chose to study marbles as merely one context in
which such knowledge was displayed.

Piaget sought to understand two aspects of the game:

First, the practice of the rules, i.e. the way in which

children of different ages apply rules; and second, the consciousness of rules, i.e. the idea which children at different ages form of the character of these game rules, whether of something obligatory and sacred or of something subject to their own choice.

As with his other research, the findings were interpreted in terms of developmental stages. This aspect of growing up in the playground, or of moral development, involves passing through each of four stages of the practice or behavioural conformity to rules. Initially the child uses the marbles simply as a free play material, not attempting to adapt his behaviour to any social rules. Between three and four years he enters stage two and begins to imitate aspects of the rule-regulated play of his elders. But although confident that he is following these older children's rules, he none the less plays in an idiosyncratic, socially-isolated manner, unintentionally flouting the rules at every turn. Stage three comes at around seven or eight when the child starts to play in a genuinely social way, in accordance with a mutually agreed set of rules. But it is only around eleven or twelve that they are completely understood and always obeyed.

As for the consciousness of rules, it is hardly surprising that during stage one of free play, the child seems to have none. During stage two some very harsh ideas about rules emerge, for now they are regarded as eternal and unchangeable, stemming from a parental or divine authority. Any suggested alterations are resisted since the new rules would be 'unfair', even if acceptable to the other players. Yet the same child who sees rules as sacred is none the less unwittingly breaking them at every turn of his actual behaviour. However, once the child begins actually to obey the rules at seven or eight, a change in attitude follows a few years later. The ten- or eleven-year-old sees them for what they are, as merely arbitrary conventions that can be changed, provided that all the players agree.

Piaget is not primarily known for his excursions into the social world of the playground, but rather for his discoveries about how children understand their physical environment. We cannot be sure whether or not he ever played marbles again, but if he did, these games were not recorded.

My own work in the playground takes up, nearly five decades later, some of the themes that Piaget first suggested. It is an attempt to understand the social world of a First and Middle School playground, through noting what the children did and said to each other, and supplementing this material through talking both to them and to their teachers. The number of children I watched is small but I came to know them well and to realize the complexities of life in their playground community. In revealing the many ways in which children talk to and manipulate each other, we are reminded not only of our own childhood, but also of everyday adult life. It is both an illuminating and amusing exercise!

2

'Hey Mister, can I be in your book?'

> *Teresa* (7): What do you use that radio for? Who are you
> speaking to with that sort of thing? Because
> it won't do you any good; unless you're
> operating for someone to smuggle us away.

Children are inevitably interested in a strange man talking into
a pocket dictaphone and walking round their playground, but
they are not nearly so self-conscious as adults. Nor is the
playground a secret society, but only a world which normally
grown-ups do not enter. Of course, the younger the children
the more easily they become accustomed to an observer. Those
who watch preschool children find that a non-participant role
causes them quickly to lose interest in an adult who never
initiates any interactions nor responds to any of the children's
attempts to make contact. This was the approach I tried in
First School and by the end of a month of pilot observation the
number of approaches by the five- and six-year-olds had
fallen dramatically to practically zero. This lack of interest
continued during the following two years of the study and even
when I observed the ten-year-olds at Middle School I was able
to stand within a few feet of them and whisper into my tape
recorder the actual words that they used, without their seeming
the least bit disturbed.

But an adult who talks to himself and refuses to interact is
something of a mystery. During the early days I was asked:

Who are you talking to?
What's that radio for?
Why are you following us about?
Why don't you answer? Why don't you answer?
Hey, you Man, speak!

Since the teachers were fairly non-committal as to why I was
there, the children soon began to proffer their own explanations:

He's a nutter.
He's a deaf man.
He's a spy.
Why are you lazy like that, why are you so lazy?
I know, I know, it's because he's tired.
He's shy, it's a radio, he's recording what we say,
I'll make him wake up.

He doesn't speak, he's a bastard.
If you don't speak, I'll just have to smack you.
I won't leave you alone, till you tell me what that
thing's for.

Within a few weeks the children became more and more
familiar with my presence and I became part of the furniture
of the playground. On one occasion they used me in a game of
'all after that man there' and for fifty seconds I was mobbed,
pulled and kicked by a bevy of five-year-olds. Happily, the
noise was more alarming than the blows and so I concluded that
this was an example of pretend fighting. On another occasion
I became incorporated into a piece of rhyming word play, as
two five-year-old girls revealed to each other my true identity.

Jane: He's about that big.
Sophie (to me): You're about that big.
Jane: He's a dum dum.
Sophie: He's daft, he's a paddy dum dum.
Jane: I know what he is, I know what he is.
Sophie: What?
Jane: He's a lazy bugger; he never gets up in the morning.

The more the children became used to me as part of the
furniture, the more I began to ask them questions as to what
they were doing. This did not disrupt their activities for they
simply replied to my questions and returned to what they had
been doing.
Whereas adopting a deaf and dumb stance was possible with
young children, it proved more difficult with the older ones at
Middle School. Not only were they more insistent with their
questions, but I felt morally obliged to treat them more like
adults, and tell them the truth. It is far from easy to stoically
ignore a delegation of thirty nine- to thirteen-year-olds
demanding, 'Can you tell us what you're doing?' I replied,
'I'm just having a look round so that I can write a book about
playtime.' The children were satisfied and left me alone, but on
another occasion a group of twelve-year-olds gathered round
chanting menacingly, 'We've got him surrounded, we've got
him surrounded.' Since it was impossible to make an excuse and
leave, I put on a brave face and joked with them. It turned out
that all they wanted to know was, 'Hey Mister, can I be in your
book?', and how could I refuse.
The fact that I was in Middle School specifically to follow up
a group of children from First School made my introduction even
easier, for the ones that knew me quickly jumped in to reassure
the others that I was harmless. When I was asked, 'Are you a
policeman?', they explained, 'No he's not, his name's Andy, he
talks to himself.'
Just as before, I was soon accepted as part of the playground
furniture. Children occasionally dared me to 'go into the girls'

toilets' but quickly disappeared before hearing my reply, and
others tried to tease me with, 'He's the detective of the year,
he's the man from Radio 2.' The children soon began to understand why I so frequently visited the playground. One morning
I was welcomed with, 'Andy, just in time for playtime. It's
lucky you're only here at playtime; you're no good at work, are
you Andy?' Compared with the younger children, the older
ones were more aware of my special interests and also more
concerned to guard their privacy. 'Hey there's a fight over
there; you love watching fights, don't you?' But when I arrived,
one of the spectators shouted, 'Get lost with your tape
recorder', though this sort of reaction was rare. By and large
the children were so engrossed in their activities that my
presence did not seem to disturb them.

THE PLAYGROUND AND THE OBSERVATIONS

I chose to observe in a small First School in a mainly working-
class area of the city. There were only one hundred five- to
eight-year-olds and the limited amount of playground space
meant that I could easily locate each one of them. Both this
school and the larger Middle School down the road for nine- to
thirteen-year-olds, to which I and some of the children in the
top class later graduated, had been built last century. They
each provided a number of adjacent tarmac areas surrounded
by railings and with relatively little play equipment, save for
lines painted on the ground for hopscotch, football and netball
and a few upturned wooden logs in the First School.
    Morning playtime lasted fifteen minutes and was supervised
by whichever teacher was unlucky enough to be on playground
duty. During the lunch hour, the children were watched over
by two 'dinner-ladies', so called throughout England because
they are employed on the same pay scales as Assistant Cooks.
Both schools had a policy to allow the children as much freedom
as possible, provided that they did not harm each other or, as
I did on my first day at school, walk out the front gate and go
home. In subsequent years guards were appointed from among
the older children to stop anyone attempting to follow my
example. In the two Oxford schools, at any rate, the dinner-
ladies were deterrent enough.
    During the first month of observation I let my eyes scan the
playground and made a note of all the different activities. Over
the next three months I used this extensive list to watch each
child over and over again for just three minutes at a time. In
this way I found out exactly what they did, with whom they did
it and how often it occurred. Watching every playtime meant
that I quickly gained an impression of life there, and during
the following two years I became more and more interested in
just one aspect of this world - the types of problems that
children meet in the playground and the various ways in which

they are solved. Because these episodes gave me so much
material to puzzle over, I made fewer visits to the playground.
For every month of daily playtime observation, three more
were needed to make full sense of my notes. Much of this book
is about how children produce solutions to everyday problems
that they meet, but in order fully to understand the significance
of those episodes, we must first have a clear picture of playtime activities in general.

The Oxford playgrounds were much the same in appearance
as the one in which I served my own apprenticeship some twenty
years ago. But times have changed and unlike that Primary
School in Leicester, the sexes were no longer kept apart in
different playgrounds, each with their own entrance marked in
bold letters BOYS and GIRLS. These led up interminable flights
of stairs to the classrooms where there was further segregation.
The boys sat on one side of the room and we were addressed by
our surnames, while the girls sat on the other and were
favoured with their first names. We did not question this imposed
segregation either in the classroom or in the playground, partly
because we had little choice in the matter and partly because
it did, to some extent, reflect our own preferences.

I have already mentioned the evidence from a whole variety of
cultures that when children are allowed to choose their own
partners, boys prefer boys and girls prefer girls. This was
also true in the Oxford playgrounds, with the preference for
interacting with the same sex increasing from 75 per cent of
all companions among the infants (five- and six-year-olds) to
85 per cent among the juniors (seven- and eight-year-olds) to
90 per cent among the nine- and ten-year-olds at Middle School.
Of course this still leaves a substantial number of cross-sex
interactions, and even at my old school we managed to play
with the girls despite the physical difficulty. Sometimes it was
skipping games in the no-man's-land between the two playgrounds, chanting rhymes that I have now completely forgotten.
Since this was such an obviously innocuous activity, it was
tacitly accepted by the teachers. But 'kiss chase' had to be a
bit more secret, and as for the exchange of views over our
developing anatomies, this only took place in the bicycle sheds
behind the church hall next door.

It is still a mystery to me just why the sexes were kept apart,
but most probably the teachers believed that boys play rough
games in large gangs which would disturb the girls' quieter
small group activities. We can see from the two Oxford schools
how this impression could arise, but it rather exaggerates the
difference between the sexes. While it is true that among the
infants, girls were more often alone and watching what everyone else was doing, both sexes spent most of their time either
by themselves or with just one or two companions. As they
grew older, all the children began to interact in larger groups,
with the boys generally preferring more companions than the
girls.

Likewise, although there were a number of differences between the boys' and girls' activities, there were also many similarities. Both sexes spent about 40 per cent of their time in play and games and the variety was striking. Not only were there many of the games so vividly described by the Opies, but in addition I noticed games of marbles, hopscotch, football, turning round and round to get dizzy, skipping and jumping, singing and clapping, dancing, gymnastic exercises, travelling piggyback style and playing with objects. But it was not all play and games; indeed, serious activities accounted for around 20 per cent of their time in the playground. I saw the boys and girls read, write, practise the recorder, teach each other, bargain, follow the directions of the teacher or simply eat and converse.

No doubt we all have highly selective memories of childhood and playtime is no exception. I particularly recall taking part in boxing matches within a ring specially created by our cast-off clothing, kicking around a tennis ball which must have laid the foundation for many a soccer star and flicking cigarette cards so as to add to my personal collection. I have no recollection whatsoever of any serious activities, nor of just standing around doing nothing, which was the way in which the children I observed spent about 10 per cent of their time.

But what of the differences in choice of activity between the sexes? The impression that boys are more boisterous fits in well with what I saw. The infant boys were four times as often involved in chasing games as the girls, and twice as often in pretend role plays, of the 'horses', 'cops and robbers' or 'Starsky and Hutch' variety. The girls, on the other hand, preferred the more sedate game of hopscotch, though a sixth of the participants were boys. Among the older children, boys specialized in soft punches and gentle strangulation, but this pretend fighting was practically absent from the girls' repertoire. Are boys more aggressive than girls? The reports from other cultures were confirmed in Oxford. The seven- and eight-year-old boys spent twice as much time teasing, arguing or fighting.

Although this difference between the sexes can be seen in streets and playgrounds throughout the world, other aspects of what children do during school playtime are far more specific to that particular context. For instance, 80 to 90 per cent of playground companions were of more or less the same age, mirroring the strict age segregation of the classroom. In contrast, children's social life outside school brings them into contact with a much wider age range. One survey conducted on the streets of a small town in the midwestern United States found that approximately 65 per cent of the children's interactions involved individuals who differed in age by at least a year.

Back in the playground, there was one curious difference between the sexes. Although all the children showed a marked

reference to stay with companions of roughly the same age,
e girls were twice as likely to play in groups with older or
nger peers. In other words, infant and junior girls more
iily interacted together than did infant and junior boys.
s this have any significance for later sex roles? Certainly,
girls more often looked after or 'mothered' the youngest
lren and this can even be seen at preschool. But just how
_ortant is such experience for future parenthood? Nobel prize
winner, Niko Tinbergen, believes that mixed age playgroups
are vital for normal development. He points to societies, such
as that of the African Bushmen, where life-styles have changed
little over the last 2000 years and children anywhere between
eighteen months and thirteen years are frequently seen
together. In these 'Third World' cultures, where women have a
major role in trading and farming, they routinely assign infant
and toddler care to their children. These 'child nurses' are
responsible for entertaining, carrying, feeding and bedding
down the infants and young children in their care. Tinbergen
suggests that in this way girls routinely learn the skills of
mothercraft and that occasional baby-sitting in modern cities
comes nowhere near to providing the same rich experience.

If Tinbergen is correct, then the girls' greater willingness
to interact with younger children might be seen in the light
of their caring role in non-industrial societies. It might
be important too in helping to ease their transition from the First
to the Middle School playground. Although both sexes showed
a temporary drop in the amount of play and games, in favour
of more serious activities such as talking, it was the boys who
seemed to be under greater stress. Unlike the girls, they
spent much of their first two weeks just standing around doing
nothing, either by themselves or in small groups. The girls had
the advantage of being able to make friends more easily across
age barriers. Indeed, the nature of their friendships may be
somewhat different from friendships among boys. It seems that
girls prefer to have just a few 'best friends' and are not so
easily worried by criticism from other children. This fits in well
with what I saw at Middle School, where the boys from very
early on continually discussed who could beat up whom and were
obviously concerned to gain approval from all their classmates.

One way in which the Oxford schools differed from my own
was in having a large proportion of children from racial
minorities. About a quarter of the pupils came from homes where
the main language was Tamil, Punjabi, Urdu or Bengali. Though
they were nearly all born in this country and were not immigrants, most had communication problems in English. When I
was growing up in Leicester, immigrants were only just beginning to arrive. Although none had reached my Church of
England school, my own non-practising Jewish background posed
the Headmaster a problem and he was never quite sure how to
treat me. On my first day in the infants, I was told to stay out
of morning assembly and the two girls with whom I had been left

explained to me that I was Jewish. It was certainly the first
I had heard of it! But as a junior, I was invited to attend
prayers 'so as not to feel different'. This both confused me and
it annoyed the other Jewish children. One of these girls took
advantage of a teacher's temporary absence from the classroom
to announce, 'There are three Jews in this class; Sarah and I
make two.' As the third I did not dare own up. I can well
understand how children from ethnic minorities are often embarrassed about being different. Unless the schools make a real
effort, these children can easily develop a poor image of their
cultural heritage.

The Oxford First School had a clear policy about how to
educate for life in a multi-racial society. Rather than ignore
racial and cultural differences and treat all the children as if
they were exactly the same, they made a conscious effort to
talk about the differences and carefully removed any books from
their library that portrayed other cultures in terms of unflat-
tering stereotypes. But, even at that school, one teacher told
me that some of the 'immigrants' do not integrate and are
excluded from games because they refuse to speak English. In
fact, my observations showed that they participated in just
the same activities as the other children and I only once heard
them 'talk in their own language' and that was an attempt by
two little girls to tease me. While it was true that they had a
slight preference for choosing friends from among other racial
minority children, this was probably because they had known
them from before starting school. Happily, we shall see that the
teachers' efforts resulted in very little racism at playtime and
of course the first common culture for all these children was that
of the playground. This has survived for many years, despite
great changes among those responsible for its transmission.

3

'Eeny, meeny, macka, racka...'

I went to a Chinese restaurant
to buy a loaf of bread,
They wrapped it up in a five-pound note
and this is what they said:
'My name is
eeny, meeny, macka, racka,
ar, I, domma, knacker,
knicker, bocker, lolli, popper,
om, pom, push.'

Many of the activities that I saw at playtime were not just made up on the spot, but had been handed down from generation to generation. 'Eeny, meeny, macka, racka ...' is just one example of this culture and my observations within only two schools revealed the continuing existence of an immensely rich folklore, despite the impression of all the teachers and dinner-ladies that such traditions were dying out. Indeed, over the years many scholars have had similar fears and have set out to collect examples of children's oral traditions so as to provide a written record of this 'dying' culture. Yet these traditional rhymes, songs and games have continued to flourish despite their imagined imminent extinction.

The same is true in countries other than our own. One recent collection called 'Cinderella Dressed in Yella' amply displays how in modern Australia, despite TV, the transistor, bingo and drive-ins, there are still two sanctuaries for the ancient traditional stories and songs - the pub and the school playground. Nearer home, even Flora Thompson was far too pessimistic in believing that the games and rhymes of her childhood during the 1880s in the hamlet of Lark Rise (Juniper Hill on the Oxfordshire/Northants border) would quickly disappear as life-styles changed:

Of all the generations that had played the games, that of the eighties was to be the last. Already those children had one foot in the national school and one on the village green. Their children and grandchildren would have left the village green behind them; new and as yet undreamed of pleasures and excitements would be theirs. In ten years time, the games would be neglected and in twenty forgotten. But all through the eighties the games went on and seemed to the children themselves and to onlookers part of a life that always had been and always would be.

As it turned out, these pastimes survived the passage from
village green to school playground. Indeed, the children in the
two Oxford schools enjoyed many of the same activities that
Flora Thompson had recorded at Lark Rise almost a hundred
years before.

CHOOSING ROLES

The children's games invariably involved the allocation of specific roles and the variety of methods available often made this
task so absorbing that the serious business of the game itself
never got under way. The Opies devote a whole chapter to
these procedures, but for the five- and six-year-old infants
that I observed, roles were usually apportioned 'in a flash';
the children either accepting a role, 'You be it', or volunteering
themselves, 'I'll be batman'.
   Amongst the juniors I saw many more ways of choosing 'it' -
usually the chaser in a game of catch. It is among this age-
group, the seven- and eight-year-olds, that the more elaborate
methods first become common though by Middle School they
seemed largely to have died out. The most popular methods
involve dipping or counting out. The players form up in a line
or circle and one of them counts along the line the number of
counts prescribed by the accented syllables of the rhyme. The
child on whom the last count falls is allocated the role under
dispute and then the game begins; or, more often, he or she is
counted 'out' and stands aside while the rhyme is repeated and
a second player eliminated, and so on, until only one player
remains and that player is the unlucky one.
   'Ip dip...' provided the opening for a whole family of counting
out rhymes:

> Ip dip fobble bip, who's it? not you.
> Ip dip sky blue, who's it? not you.
> Ip dip dog shit, who stepped in it?
> Ippy dippy dation,
> my operation,
> how many people at the station?
> you are not 'it'.

I also heard the well known rhyme:

> Eeny, meeny, miney, mo,
> catch a knicker by the toe,
> if it squeals, let it go,
> eeny, meeny, miney, mo.

Happily, the racist version that I knew as a child has now
disappeared; 'nigger' having given way to 'knicker'. This
single word has brought in its wake an even newer variation of

the rhyme in which the middle lines have been replaced by 'lost my knickers in the snow; if you find them let us know'.

Although 'eeny, meeny, miney, mo' starts with what appears to be complete gibberish, there are other rhymes that continue in this vein. I have already mentioned:

Eeny, meeny, macka, racka,
ar, I, domma, knacker,
knicker, bocker, lolli, popper,
om, pom, push.

The Opies record a slightly different version of the introduction to this rhyme. Their loaf of bread is purchased at a Chinese laundry rather than at a restaurant but is more sensibly wrapped in a tablecloth and not a five pound note. It appears that the recital of this rhyme has a history far beyond the First School playground in which I heard it. According to the Opies, children know it as 'Chinese counting' and use this piece of gibberish, with or without its introduction, to choose roles before a game. The words show surprisingly little variation throughout the English-speaking world.

How the dip came to be called 'Chinese counting' or how the rhyme itself arose remains a mystery, but it appears to have been a relatively recent invention. In the Opies' collection of over a thousand separate recordings of gibberish counting out rhymes, this one only came into play during the 1920s. Before then children favoured other nonsense rhymes, but many of them contained elements of our own contemporary 'eeny, meeny, macka, racka', that nowadays reigns supreme in British playgrounds. They write:

The theory that these rhymes are centuries old is not to be lightly dismissed. It will ever be a wonder that children who cannot remember their eight-times table for half-an-hour, can nevertheless carry in their heads assemblages of rhythmical sounds, and do so with such constancy that gibberish remains recognizable although repeated in different centuries, in different countries, and by children speaking different languages.

Not only are these rhymes handed down from child to child, but direct teaching by parents or even grandparents may serve to secure their survival over the decades. Eight-year-old Clare told me that she learnt the following rhyme from her grandmother:

Ar, ar, chickerah,
roney, poney,
pom, pom, piney
hari, gari, gasha,
Chinese Sea.

This is obviously a continuation of a rhyme that even in the
1890s stretched from Scotland to the United States; the Opies
record two versions:

Ra, ra, chuckeree, chuckeree,
ony, pony,
ningy, ningy, na,
addy, caddy, westce,
anty, poo,
chutipan, chutipan,
China, chu.
(Fraserburgh 1891)

Rye, chy, chookereye,
  chookereye,
choo, choo, ronee, ponee,
icky, picky, nigh,
caddy, paddy, vester,
canlee, poo,
itty pau, jutty pau,
Chinee Jew.
(Pennsylvania 1897)

Dips that are relatively short are open to manipulation for the
participants might count ahead. Evidence that I collected in an
experimental study suggests that children begin to realize this
possibility at about eight years, indeed soon after rhymes start
to be commonly used. It cannot be known whether or not
participation dips arose in order to safeguard against such
manipulation, but making the child add a word or number in
the middle of the dip does offer some protection.
    The following participation dip was by far the most popular
in the playgrounds.

Racing car, racing car, number nine,
using petrol all the time;
how many gallons did he lose?
(The person the count falls on says a number, perhaps
THREE, and this is counted out, ONE, TWO, THREE).

This seems to be an updated form of the rhyme mentioned by
the Opies as current in the United States at the height of the
railroads:

Engine, engine, number nine,
running on the Chicago line,
when she's polished, she will shine,
engine, engine, number nine.

Manipulation can best be prevented by dips where the participation still leaves a sizeable section of the rhyme to be counted
out. This is the case with the following dip that an eight-year-
old boy introduced into First School playground. The Opies
trace it back to 1898.

As I was walking down the inky pinky lane,
I met three inky pinky children,
they asked me this and they asked me that,
they asked me the colour of the Union Jack,
red, white or blue?
BLUE

blue is the beauty, the beauty, the beauty,
blue is the beauty, you are not it.

The junior children also used methods to choose 'it' that even
more obviously relied on a particular skill. Often the outcome
depended on some ability such as running fast or physical
strength. A child might shout, 'Last one to the wall is "it"' or
'First one to put a foot in the drain is "it".' In the latter, boys
all joined hands in a circle and tried to pull each other with so
much force that one of their number would let a foot fall onto
the drain, around which the circle had formed. These methods
were rarer than dipping, however, and on one occasion I even
heard a touch of true democracy among a group of girls: 'Who
hasn't been "it"? Put their hands up!'

It would be tempting to believe that the counting out rhymes
rely solely on chance, in contrast to the skilled methods above.
According to the Opies, 'Most children prefer the allotment of
the disliked role to be a matter of chance. They feel that if
the choice has been made by providence then there is no
possibility of argument.' But observations in Philadelphia by
Kenneth Goldstein of how children actually dip shows the
situation to be more complicated. Almost 90 per cent of the
children told Goldstein that counting out was a game of chance,
but field-work revealed that it was not. Rather, it was a game
of strategy, in which the rhymes and movements of the players
were manipulated to limit or remove chance as a factor in
selection. Goldstein observed six methods of cheating: extend-
ing the rhyme was most common, the others were selecting a
rhyme with the right number of stresses, skipping over regular
counts, designating either the first or last person to be 'it',
changing position in the circle and, lastly, obtaining respite
by calling out 'safe'. My own observations of eight-year-olds
counting out suggests that when among their peers, children
claim that dipping involves chance, but many told me privately
that these dips can be manipulated. Indeed, for many children
this seemed an important discovery and one to be kept secret
from their less aware playmates. Armed with this knowledge
they were free to accuse others of cheating, whilst indulging
in the same practices themselves.

Some rhymes not only selected roles, but were repeated as an
integral part of the game. A group of girls all stood in a line
with their palms outstretched. One of their number proceeded
down the line slapping each hand in turn to the syllables of:

Hop, hop, hop, to the golliwog's shop,
to see how long it takes you,
and when you get there,
your mother will say,
stop chasing the boys from the USA,
how dare you disobey me.

The girl on whom the last count landed immediately had to shout 'stop' as the 'slapper' ran away from the others. The rhyme was now repeated by the selected girl, who became the 'hopper', since she had to hop back and forth between the children still in the line and the 'slapper'. The choice of length of hop was critical for, if on the last syllable the 'hopper' could touch the 'slapper' without having to move, then the two swapped roles. The enjoyment of the game seemed to derive more from watching the hopping and the slapping than from any element of competition.

Interestingly, the Opies record a similar rhyme but it is chanted in a different context. Here it is a way of selecting two boys to take part in a 'cock-fight'; that is, a fight in which they must both try to knock each other over whilst balancing on one leg.

Hop, hop, hop, to the butcher's shop,
I dare not stay no longer,
for if I do my mother will say,
I've been with the boys down yonder.

Lastly, a method not of choosing roles before a game starts, but of deciding which of two captains in a football match should be allowed first choice or 'pick'. Subsequently the selection alternated between the two until the teams reached full complement. In 'hammer and nails' the two captains stood at a distance of about twenty feet apart and then walked towards each other at the same rate, placing each foot directly in front of the last one. When they neared the mid-point, almost always only one of the two was able to place his foot fully on the ground in the space between them. This captain was awarded first 'pick'.

CHASING GAMES[1]

Chasing games, in which a player tries to touch others who are running freely, were immensely popular among all age groups, but particularly with the infant boys. The simplest and most common were 'tig' and 'off-ground tig'. In both games the chaser had to touch another child and so pass on the 'it' or the 'dreaded lurgi', while in 'off-ground tig' temporary immunity could be obtained by clambering onto somewhere above ground level. According to the Opies, the initial source of infection of the 'dreaded lurgi' was 9 November 1954 edition of 'The Goon Show'. It has a lot to answer for!

In 'budge' the juniors elaborated on these rules, for now only one child at a time was allowed in a single safe place; the arrival of a newcomer shouting 'budge' forced the former to move.

[1] The game names that appear in brackets are the ones that the Opies give as most common throughout the British Isles.

In 'TV tig' safety was assured differently, by bobbing down
and saying the name of a TV programme. Other chasing games
did not even include this possibility, though there were a
variety of ways in which the touch might be passed on, or
restrictions as to where or how the players could proceed.
'Ball tig' involved the chaser in throwing a ball so as to hit
another child and so transmit the 'it'. In 'bogey tig' a 'bit of
snot' was extracted from the nostril and carefully placed on the
victim's person, who not unnaturally was eager to gain revenge
in the same distasteful manner.

The connection between bogey and snot seems to be more
than mere coincidence. Raymond Briggs records the following
traditional rhyme in his book 'Fungus the Bogeyman':

> Scab and matter custard,
> snot and bogey pie,
> dead dog's giblets,
> green cat's eye,
> spread it on with bread,
> spread it on thick,
> wash it all down,
> with a cup of cold sick.

In 'hospital tig' (French touch) the chaser had to run
around holding onto the part of the body that had been touched;
in 'loo tig' movement was restricted to the area of the toilets
and was thus predominantly a single-sex game, while in 'line
tig' the players could only walk along the netball lines. Hopping was mandatory in 'hopping tig', as was riding astride
another in 'piggyback tig', while in 'block tig' the chaser
counted to ten as the others ran around the block, leaving 'it'
to follow in the same direction.

There were yet more variations and these concern the
consequences of being tigged. In 'scarecrow tig' (stick-in-
the-mud) a player who has been caught had to stand still
with outstretched arms awaiting the freeing hand of a child
who had not likewise been transfixed. The object here was
for 'it' to be surrounded by motionless and hence impotent
companions. 'Bear wolf' was a similar game in which the
punishment on being tigged was to sit on the wall rather than
stand still, but release could still be obtained in the same
way. Lastly, I saw 'chain-he' in which a player, having been
caught, joined hands with the chaser and as the game
progressed, so too did the length of the chain of children
running after those still at liberty.

In some catching games part of the sport is that the players
do not know when the chaser is going to begin chasing. One
such game that I saw at Middle School started with a set
dialogue:

Children: Good morning Mrs Brown.
Mrs Brown: Good morning children.
Children: What are you making?
Mrs Brown: A stew.
Children: What are you putting in it?

Mrs Brown was allowed to own up to any ingredients, e.g. 'eggs, drainpipes, spiders', but when she said 'brownies' then all the children ran away and Mrs Brown attempted to catch at least one of them. Having done so, the game started again with the same allocation of roles. I heard that this game was first played at Brownies and then recreated by a group of girls in the playground. Lastly, let us not forget 'kiss chase' which was popular with children of all ages. The sexes chased each other so as to plant upon them the ultimate embarrassment of a kiss.

CATCHING GAMES

In these games the object is for one player to attempt to intercept other players who are obliged to move from one designated area to another. 'British bulldog' is one such game and it was particularly popular among the older boys at First School. Usually some of the infants watched and occasionally a few joined in or they started a game for themselves. In 'British bulldog' there were two safe areas at opposite ends of the playground. The children gathered at one end and the 'bulldog' stood in the middle. When he called 'British bulldog, one, two, three' the players all tried to cross to the opposite safe area. Should an individual be touched by the 'bulldog', then he joined him in the middle and as their numbers increased, so it became harder and harder to effect a safe passage.

'Jack, Jack, may we cross the water?' (farmer, farmer, may we cross your golden water?) was another catching game that I saw in the playground. The Opies say that 'this is probably the most popular game in the streets of Britain today, being fascinating to little girls, partly, it seems, because of the way it draws attention to item after item of their clothing.' One child was named Jack and stood in the middle of the playground while the rest lined up at their side. These children called out:

Jack, Jack, may we cross the water?
Mummy's gone, father's gone, and I want to come too.

Jack held sole powers to let children come over and exercised his discretion according to what colour they were wearing, announcing, for example, 'only if you're wearing blue'.

SEEKING GAMES

The infants played a version of 'hide and seek' in which one
child attempted to locate others who had hidden, but upon so
doing, the whole group invariably collapsed into giggles. The
more complicated game of 'ay-ickie' (block), or as some
children called it, 'ay-ockie', was specifically a junior game.
    'Ay-ickie' involved many stages. First, the children chose a
suitable location for the starting place; in this playground it
was always the same drainpipe. Then, one child took on the
role of seeker and a ritual commenced in order to decide the
number to which he or she had to count whilst facing the
drainpipe with eyes closed. The other children all joined hands
and together made as if to touch the back of the seeker, but
in reality only one of these many fingers had made contact.
They now asked in unison, 'Who did the dot?', and the seeker
turned round to face a semi-circle of outstretched hands.
For every wrong hand the count had to increase from zero to
ten, and even once the correct hand had been located, every
wrong finger suffered the same penalty. The final number was
doubled by saying out loud, for example, 'Fifty, double it,
is a hundred' and the count could commence as the others
rushed off to hide. The Opies do not mention this particular
prelude to hide and seek, but they do describe similar ones
such as, 'I draw a snake upon your back', that have the same
effect of deciding the time during which hiding can take place.
    When the counting was done, the seeker always cried out,
'Coming ready or not' and this tradition takes different forms
throughout the country. In Leicestershire, for example, they
announce:

> I hold my little finger,
> I thought it was my thumb,
> I give you all a warning,
> and here I come.

Should an individual be spotted, then the seeker had to run
back to the drainpipe and shout 'ay-ickie (John)'. Should John
manage to arrive at the drainpipe first he could shout 'ay-ickie-
in' and in this way gain safety. When all the children had
either been 'ay-ickied' or 'ay-ickied-in' then the game recom-
menced and the first child to have been caught became the new
seeker.
    Lastly, I saw the following curious game only at Middle
School. A group of girls stood in a column, each with her
arms on the shoulders of the girl in front and covering this
person's eyes with her hands. As the column walked along, it
gradually diminished in number as individuals went off to hide.
In this way the girl at the front of the column was left with
the task of looking for all those who had disappeared. Invariably, however, the game turned into a giggling session rather

than a systematic search.

RACING GAMES

Races were rare among the infants but when they did take
place the whole length of the playground might be turned into
a race track. The juniors, but not the Middle School children,
spent much more time in competitive racing. During 1976 the
winning by a Briton of the World Racing Car Championship
was celebrated with 'James Hunt races' and there were separate
knock-out heats for the boys and girls. Timed races were
another variant during which each child set out separately on
a course, while the others kept the time by either consulting a
watch or by counting aloud, at a speed that seemed to depend
on who was running.

There were three racing games played by children of all
ages, but in particular by the girls, in which the progress of
those taking part depended on their fulfilling a condition. In
'Mother may I?' players could only move forward according to
the instructions that they received individually from the one
in front who employed a terminology more or less peculiar to
this game, thus: 'Jean, take one giant and three baby steps',
'Pauline, do a lamppost', 'Phil, five pigeon steps'. The player
addressed asked 'May I?' and advanced as instructed, then
waited where she was until her turn came again. However,
should a player forget to ask 'May I?' and advance before
receiving permission, she had to go back to the starting line.
Many of the children that I observed played more simply, dis-
carding the restriction of having to ask 'May I?', since for
them the enjoyment seemed to lie most in the actual dialogue
and contorted movements that might be demanded.

A second game, again popular within a wide age range, was
'grandmother's footsteps'. It has many different names throughout the country; the Opies give its name in Oxford as
'Policemen' and claim curiously that 'grandmother's footsteps'
is restricted to private schools. In this game the children could
only take steps over a prescribed course when the grandmother
had her back turned. Should she spy anyone moving when she
periodically turned round, then that player had to go back
and start again. The third racing game with wide appeal was
'red letter', in which progress forward by one step was
conditional upon the participants' names containing the letter
that was called out.

A number of games that Middle School girls played involved
only two competitors running against each other at a time, one
of them generally being instrumental in the selection of the
other. In 'white horses' all but one of the players lined up along
a wall and each child took a name from a particular class of
names, i.e. TV programmes, pop stars, etc. The other person
was 'it' and was told these names, but not which individuals

held them. She called out a name at random and the person so
selected had to race against her to the opposite wall and back,
shouting 'white horses' on her return. The winner became the
new 'it'. If the class of names was games, then the children
called this variation 'polo'; when the names were illnesses, then
this collective noun alone sufficed.

'We are the ostriches' (bump-on-the-back) was another game
that the Middle School girls played. The children gathered in a
circle and one of their number - the lion - ran round the outside, while the other chanted, 'we are the ostriches, see how
they run, the lion is a-coming, and it's time for fun.' On the
last word the lion tapped one of the ostriches on the back and
so started a race. The lion ran in one direction and the ostrich
in the other; the first one to get back to the vacant space
was allowed to join or remain in the circle.

'Oxford and Cambridge' no doubt maintains its interest in
Oxford because of the traditional competition between the two
towns. I only saw this game at Middle School, but it was very
popular there. The two teams sat on the ground facing each
other and each pair, touching by the soles of their feet, was
given a number (or a label of some sort, like the name of a
shop). Another child outside these teams (presumably the
referee) called out the number of the pair and also specified
the number of circuits that they had to run, each circuit taking
them first behind and then over the legs of the other children.
The first one back to his or her starting position scored a
point for the team.

Lastly, there was another much simpler type of race at
Middle School. In 'express' one child turned toward the drainpipe and counted up to a specific number. The others took up
a stance only a few yards away. When the counter turned
round he or she had to touch at least one player, who then took
over that role. To avoid this possibility, the children could
become immune by quickly touching the drainpipe.

DUELLING AND EXERTING GAMES

In some games, two players place themselves in direct conflict
with each other and often the qualities of most account are
physical strength and stamina. For example, I occasionally
observed 'lolly sticks' among the infants. Each of two children
took turns in holding out their used lollipop sticks, which the
opponent tried to break in half using the stick as an axe.
There were also a few 'piggyback fights' among children of
this age.

'Roll over, roll over, Karen's coming over' was the chant of
one team of five-year-olds, all holding hands in a line. Karen
ran across and threw herself against the line of children
opposite her, who took up the chant and propelled one of their
number back in exchange. The Opies call this game 'red rover'

and claim that it is only rarely found in England, but is a
favourite of Scottish schoolgirls. Should a child break through
the line then he or she can return to his own team, but a
failure to run through meant joining the team that had made
the capture. For infants this game seemed to lack any competitive element, while the juniors and Middle School children
played much more fiercely.

I often wondered how and why the nature of the game changes
between five and ten years. My friend, William Maxwell, has
some striking observations from an Edinburgh School which
point to the need for the older children to teach the younger
ones that being rough can also be fun. He saw an older ten-
year-old boy in among a group of half a dozen five-year-olds.
The younger ones were playing gently, as in Oxford, but the
older boy, however, was instructing them to break through the
line of linked arms. At first they appeared bewildered but they
soon caught on.

New versions of a game are not automatically taken up by the
community unless they have some added attraction. This was
the problem which the older boy faced. To begin with, the little
ones remained unamused when attempts were made to break
through the line and they just looked at each other nervously,
even when the attempts failed. The ten-year-old had to make
them realize that such attempts were really rather funny. After
every run he would laugh loudly and did so in an exaggerated
manner. After several such outbursts, the younger boys began
to display similar amusement. William Maxwell points out that
this lad spent about half an hour teaching the younger ones and
this was in sharp contrast to the impression he gave of being
a 'tough' and far from patient individual.

There were three exerting games which only the juniors
played. The first was 'leapfrog' in which children jumped over
the backs of others crouching down. The second was known in
this playground as 'round-the-circle' but by the Opies as
'adders' nest'. The children, mainly boys, formed a circle by
joining hands and at a given signal each player tried, without
breaking the circle, to force one or other of his neighbours to
place a foot inside a small centre circle painted on the ground
for netball matches. This game was occasionally used to choose
who's 'it', but more often played for its own sake. An interesting game which the Opies do not mention is called 'mercy' and
strangely attracted only girls. Pairs of children interlocked
the fingers of each hand and squeezed as hard as possible.
The aim was for one child to be in so much pain that she had
to shout 'mercy' at which the other immediately let go and
found a new contestant. The concept of mercy is not totally
unknown in children's folklore; in 'mercy touch' which is
played in the West Country 'you kneel on the ground and
say mercy' in order to obtain temporary immunity.

DARING GAMES

I noticed a few daring games that all involved an element of
risk. One of these was a pastime that I have called 'falling
forwards' since it did not appear that the children gave it a
name. One child stood against the wall while the other stood
in front with his or her arms outstretched and pointing at the
first one's eyes. The daring aspect came in when this child
fell forward and only removed the fingers from their threatening position at the very last moment. The child accepting the
dare tried hard not to blink or would suffer being called a
'scarebaby'.

The Opies classify 'follow-the-leader' as a daring game and
it was very popular among the junior girls. However, there
was rarely any daring aspect since the leader, a role which
never changed hands during my observation period, seemed
content to be followed without making them perform any
dangerous tricks.

GUESSING GAMES

A very simple guessing game, popular among children of all
ages, was to creep up behind a friend, cover his or her eyes
with your hands, and demand, 'Who is it?'; it is an enjoyable
pastime that attracts even adults. A much more complicated
guessing game was 'coloured eggs' in which juniors and infants
played together. One child became the mother, another the
big bad wolf, and the rest were eggs and had to choose a
colour. The wolf, who had not been party to their selection,
came to the door and knocked. He asked, 'Have you any
coloured eggs?', and the mother replied, 'What colour?'; the
wolf named a colour. If there were no eggs of that colour
everybody stood firm and the wolf had to go away and try
again; but if one of the players had assumed this colour, he
had to run for his life in a circle around the playground. Should
this one be caught, then he took the place of the big bad wolf,
but if he managed to return home, then he was safe. The
renowned 'postman's knock', curiously not mentioned by Opies,
is similar to 'coloured eggs' but involved kissing the child
whose number, rather than colour, is correctly guessed.

In 'TV initials' the object of the game was to guess the name
of a television programme from only a limited amount of information. For example, one child stood in front of the others and
announced, 'It's NW and on BBC 1 at 6.00 p.m. Mondays
to Fridays'. The child who recognized this programme had to
run to the announcer and back twice, before correctly guessing
'Nationwide' and the two swapped roles.

'Queenie' [the Opies write] is the perpetual delight of little
girls aged eight and nine [I saw it in the Middle School only]

for it has the great recommendation of combining the
mysterious pleasure of guessing with the ball-play to which
they are so much addicted. One girl is selected 'Queenie',
given the ball, and stands with her back turned to the rest.
Without looking behind her, she throws the ball back over
her head, and the other girls scramble for it. They then form
up in a row, with their hands behind their backs so that the
girl in front will not know which of them has the ball; and
they let 'Queenie' know they are ready by addressing her,
'Queenie, Queenie, where is the ball?' 'Queenie' then turns
round and picks out the player who she thinks is concealing
the ball. If her guess is correct she remains 'Queenie'; if
she is wrong, the girl who has been successful in concealing
the ball takes her place.

MARBLES AND HOPSCOTCH

Traditional games in the playground nearly always involve the
minimum of special equipment. For marbles all that is required
are a few round glass balls which can easily be purchased for
a few pence. This game was only played at First School and it
took place on grilles that were in fact drain covers. There were
two variations; 'friendlies' in which the winner returned the
marbles that had been won at the end of the match, and
'keepsies' where there was no such gentlemanly agreement.
Although marbles is often thought of as a boys' game, two-
thirds of the players were girls.

Hopscotch was still predominantly a girl's game, but one sixth
of the players at First School were boys. Any number of children could join in and the essence of the game was to throw a
stone to land in the squares marked 1 to 10, progressing up the
numerical order with each throw. On a successful throw the
player had to hop down the squares to the one in which the
stone had landed, and be careful not to step in it or touch the
lines separating the squares. It is perhaps worth wondering
whether children learn anything whilst playing hopscotch. I
often saw the very youngest four-year-olds being taught how
to play by their older companions. Surely this experience
provides them good practice in counting and recognizing numbers.

SINGING, DANCING AND HAND CLAPPING

Yet another aspect of the playground world is the extensive
stock of rhymes and songs that I mainly heard girls recite. They
usually emphasized the rhyming aspects, even to the neglect of
ensuring good sense:

Adam and Eve went down to tea,
locked the door and turned the key.

Long legged Italy,
kicked little Sicily,
In the middle of the Mediterranean Sea,
along came Germany,
feeling very Hungary,
took a bit of Turkey,
and dipped it in Greece.

Sometimes the songs were accompanied by a dance, as with
the nursery rhymes that I saw the very youngest children act
out. There was 'the farmer's in the dell' and 'ring-a-ring-a-
roses' (in which the line 'we all fall down' records the events
of the Bubonic Plague) and the following less well known one:

Daddy's in the saucer,
mummy's in the cup,
daddy's in the saucer,
we all jump up.

The older girls at Middle School had their own more complicated
favourites and these were the party games of 'a hunting we will
go' and 'in and out of the dusty bluebells'.
   Hand clapping is a highly skilled performance which involves
elaborate sequences. The simplest was for two girls to stand
opposite each other and clap, first with the left hand, then with
the right and then with both hands. Some of these songs were
quite short:

A sailor went to sea, sea, sea,
to see what he could see, see, see,
and all that he could see, see, see,
was the bottom of the deep blue sea, sea, sea.

Under the bramble bushes down by the sea,
true love for you my darling, true love for me,
and when we're married, we'll raise a family,
a boy for you and a girl for me,
under the chesnut tree.

Others were longer:

Miss Mary Black, Black, Black,
all dressed in black, black, black,
with silver buttons, buttons, buttons,
all down her back, back, back,
she asked her mother, mother, mother,
for fifty cents, cents, cents,
to see the elephants, elephants, elephants,

jump the fence, fence, fence,
they jumped so high, high, high,
they reached the sky, sky, sky,
and came back on the fifth of July.

Counting from one upwards provided the basis for the following
song:

When I was one, I sucked my thumb,
over the Irish Sea,
with a bottle of rum to warm my tum,
yes that's the life for me.

At two I lost my shoe, at three I cut my knee and so the sad
story with its comforting chorus continued, each number bringing greater and greater improvisation.
    Numbers were also involved in the crude song below. It is
one that is normally reserved for the showers after a rugby
match, but I heard it performed by two eight-year-old girls as
they clapped their hands in time:

This is number ONE and the story's just begun,
CHORUS
Roll me over, lay me down and do it again,
Roll me over in the clover,
Roll me over, lay me down and do it again.
This is number TWO and I'm telling it to you ...
This is number THREE and she's got me on her knee ...
This is number FOUR and she's got me on the floor ...
This is number FIVE and her legs are open wide ...
This is number SIX and she's pulling down her knicks ...
This is number SEVEN and it feels like we're in heaven ...
This is number EIGHT and the vicar's at the gate ...
This is number NINE and the twins are doing fine ...

Recounting some of the stages of life while hand clapping was
indeed a popular theme:

Oh Susie was a baby, a baby Susie was,
she went like this and she sucked her thumb.

Then Susie was at nursery, at nursery Susie was,
she went like this (puts her hands over her eyes) she went
    A, B, and ABC.

When Susie was a junior, a junior Susie was,
she went Miss, Miss, I can't do this.

Then Susie was a senior, a senior Susie was,
she went ooh, aah, I've lost my bra, I don't know where my
    knickers are.

(alternative verse:

> When Susie was a teenager, a teenager Susie was,
> she left her bra in her boyfriend's car and doesn't know where
> her knickers are.)

> When Susie was a mother, a mother Susie was,
> she went rock, rock, and rock, rock, rock.

> When Susie was a grandmother, a grandmother Susie was,
> she went now, now, and now, now, now.

> When Susie was a ghost, a ghost Susie was,
> she went ooh, ooh, and ooh, ooh, ooh.

But the sequence was not always from baby to ghost; in the
next story the children acted out the progression from being a
little boy or girl to a little angel in heaven.

> I'm the little Dutch girl, Dutch girl, Dutch girl,
> I'm the little Dutch girl far from the sea.

> I'm the little Dutch boy, Dutch boy, Dutch boy,
> I'm the little Dutch boy far from the sea.

> Go away I hate you, hate you, hate you,
> Go away I hate you far from the sea.

> Because you stole my necklace, my necklace, my necklace,
> Because you stole my necklace far from the sea.

> Here is your necklace, your necklace, your necklace,
> Here is your necklace far from the sea.

> Now we're getting married, married, married,
> Now we're getting married far from the sea.

> Now we've got a baby, a baby, a baby,
> Now we've got a baby far from the sea.

> Now we're up in heaven, in heaven, in heaven,
> Now we're up in heaven far from the sea.

> Now we're little angels, angels, angels,
> Now we're little angels far from the sea.

Why are children so fascinated with these tales of life? Perhaps
they are just beginning to reflect on the concepts that these
songs involve, such as birth, death, childhood and adulthood.
They must be learning here as well as in many other situations
just what is expected from little boys and little girls. But I am

sure that the five-year-old boy who told a female playmate:

> Humpty Dumpty sat on a wall,
> ate a black banana,
> where do you think he put this in,
> down a girl's pyjama.

did not realize the full implications of his words.

Nor should we assume that when the two eight-year-old girls sang 'Roll me over lay me down and do it again', they were recounting their own sexual adventures. But alas adult ears are only too easily shocked by what their children say and some in Australia even believed that they could be corrupted by their own offspring. Ten years ago the first edition of 'Cinderella Dressed in Yella' was officially denied transmission through Australian mail because of its alleged obscenity and only its research value saved it. Even the second edition has a wonderfully ironic note on its dustcover, 'Not recommended for children', when of course its real authors are the countless generations of children themselves and their traditions go way beyond the numerous games and songs that I saw at playtime. Not only do they learn these, but they must also learn how to cope with a continual stream of social problems, and it is these skills that I shall examine next.

4

'Bagsee no bagsees'

Whilst playing 'schools', six-year-old Fiona demands:

'Bagsee Teacher,
you be the children;
turn around, turn around,
you like me!'

Just as the problem of who becomes 'it' in a game of tig can be
solved by age-old methods of counting out, so too can a role
be secured with the word 'bagsee'. The Opies claim that 'bags'
or 'bagsee', which is the Oxford variation, appears to be in
general use throughout Britain and it is a word of tremendous
power. 'Bagsee mine' gains possession, 'bagsee me first' claims
precedence and 'bagsee me not it' avoids a role.
   'Bagsee' is effective because it has a clear meaning within
the playground community. It is an example of verbal ritual;
formulae that have an established meaning and do not need
further explanation or supplementary threats. But what playground rituals are there? Which problems do they solve and how
do children learn to use them?

'BAGSEE', 'CRUCEMS', 'TAXI' AND OTHER PLAYGROUND
RITUALS

The simplest rituals are single words. In addition to 'bagsee',
I heard 'crucems' and 'taxi' and these also have far-reaching
effects. 'Crucems' is a local Oxford word which enables you to
drop out of a game for a period. In other parts of the country
children employ words such as 'barley, cree, crosses, keys,
kings, fainites, scribs and skinch', all uttered whilst the child
crosses the fore and first finger of each hand.
   'Taxi' and its associated sign also solves a problem. Before
saying 'taxi' at First School, the thumb must be dabbed on the
tongue, and placed on the forehead with the palm outstretched,
or sometimes folded. The child who does this ritually denies
that he or she was responsible for passing wind and the others
in the group quickly follow suit. In Middle School the gesture
is far simpler for only the thumb and outstretched palm placed
on the bridge of the nose is retained. The meaning, however,
is completely reversed for now it is the child who farts who
needs to say 'taxi'. Should he or she fail to utter this word,

then any companions are liable to say 'sixes' and punch the offender six times, or even double the dose with 'twelves'. One child told me that similar protection is afforded by the word 'buses' should you burp.

Teachers that I talked to had all suffered sudden outbreaks of 'taxi' during their lessons but although puzzled, they had never stopped to inquire as to the word's significance. I was happy to enlighten them. Just like crucems, 'taxi' may have geographical boundaries for although it seems to be known by many Oxford children, I recently came across its equivalent 'jets' during a visit to a Battersea school. Whilst listening to their teacher, a group of seven-year-olds all successively denied farting; each said 'jets' and touched the thigh of the next person in the circle with the tips of two outstretched fingers.

Since 'bagsee' and 'crucems' were by far the most frequent rituals that I heard at playtime, I shall look more closely at the way they are used and how they come to be mastered. But these two words are only the tip of the iceberg; the Opies devote a whole chapter to such 'codes of oral legislation', of which the following are just a small selection.

To affirm that you are telling the truth, a child may offer 'God's honour', or, 'may I drop down dead if I'm telling a lie'. Alternatively, in parts of Wales, 'criss-cross' may be cried on its own or in conjunction with 'my heart' or 'my throat'. All these are effective by themselves to affirm. If there can still be any doubt about a person's veracity, however, he is liable to be tested. He may be asked, 'What will you eat?', and have to reply 'fire and brimstone'; or 'What will you do if it's not true?', suggests the response 'Tread on hot needles'. These words ritually assure the affirmation.

Making a bargain can also be achieved through the use of ritual words. The children may call out: 'It's a deal', 'Done', 'On', 'Fair enough', 'Quits', 'Double quits', 'Square', 'Eeks' and no going back on an offer is possible once it has been accepted by someone using whichever phrase is recognized as binding in his school.

To ensure anyone wanting to go back on the chief type of bargaining at school - the swap - there are a number of traditional sayings: '"No backs" in Kirkcaldy, "Tin tacks, no backs" in Peterborough, and in Croydon they hook their little fingers and shake, chanting "Touch teeth, touch leather, No backs for ever and ever".'

'BAGSEE', 'CRUCEMS' AND ORDER

The use of 'bagsee' and 'crucems' enables a child to predict better what will happen next. For instance, an individual who makes a request but omits the word 'bagsee' cannot be sure what the reactions of the others will be. In the two episodes below, the orderly apportioning of roles afforded by the use of 'bagsee'

can be contrasted with disagreement and the need to resort to
the possibly less reliable method of autocracy, when the same
group omits the word.

Mary (8:9) brings out a skipping rope:[1]
Graeme (9:3) : Bagsee me go first.
Pete (9:4) : Bagsee me go next.
John (8:8) : Bagsee me hold the rope.

A few minutes later:

Graeme : I'm in first.
Pete : I'm in with you.
Graeme : No, you're not.
Mary : I say who's going in.

I heard 'bagsee' used not only to gain possession, claim
precedence and avoid a role, but also to state extra rules in a
game. In all these contexts, the ritual makes life more predictable and acts to the advantage of the child who invokes it. If
you are repeatedly chased by the 'bulldog' in 'British bulldog',
it helps to shout 'bagsee-no-following' so that 'he can't keep
coming after you'. If you want to bide time before running
across, it helps to claim 'bagsee no guarding' so that 'he can't
stand over you till you leave the circle'. But in return the
'bulldog' might invoke 'bagsee counting' and 'if you haven't left
the safety of the ring by the time he reaches ten, then he can
come in and tig you'. And if you are about to be caught, then
jump up and shout 'bagsee-no-tigging in the air'.

'Crucems' too can bring an advantage over others. The child
who uses the word expects to gain temporary immunity in a
game for some legitimate reason, such as 'doing up a shoe lace'
or 'going to the toilet'. Yet one little girl told me that she
would say 'crucems' when she didn't need to go to the toilet
and never arrived there, but instead walked calmly past the
'bulldog' with her fingers crossed and so avoided being tigged.

Many other games also have the possibility of invoking addi-
tional rules which modify or cancel the basic regulations.
Although it was usual in the Oxford playgrounds to preface any
such request with 'bagsee', this powerful formula does not
appear to be necessary in games or marbles. One former player
from the mid-1940s in Yorkshire recalls how experienced
participants would bewilder their opponents by adroit manipulation of conventions such as 'no-drops', 'no-cannons', 'no-brush',
'no-sweeps' and 'no-hard-fires'. But having a flexible rule
structure does not only benefit the skilful player. Rivka
Eifermann has studied the variations of marbles popular with
Israeli children and she often saw six-year-olds invoke rules

[1] The numbers in brackets are the children's ages in years
and months.

which simplify the game so that they too could join in with the ten-year-olds, whilst playing at a level of challenge more fitted to their abilities.

'BAGSEE', 'CRUCEMS' AND LEARNING ABOUT THEIR POWER

One of the most noticeable features of the First School playground was the nearly total absence of 'bagsee', 'crucems' and 'taxi' from the speech of the five- and six-year-olds. It was the seven- and eight-year-olds who used these words, but at Middle School they were once again less common. How do the children become adept in using these rituals? It is no surprise to learn that children teach each other about the social power of these new words. Should an individual ignore the ritual, he or she may be put right as to its meaning. For example, 'Don't keep coming and tigging me if I've got crucems' or the following exchange:

Cheryl (9:4):   Bagsee no tigging back.
Bridget (8:3): She tug me and I tug her back.
Cheryl: Ah well, you're still 'it' then.

But if teaching is such a simple task, why do the five-year-olds not learn more quickly? Although their games are fairly simple they still have ample opportunity to practise these rituals. The answer lies perhaps in realizing that learning 'bagsee' and 'crucems' involves a number of stages and the six-year-old Duncan in the next episode is only part the way there.

In a game of off-ground tig:
Matthew (6:8): I've got crucems, I've got crucems.
Alan (5:4):   We've got crucems.
Duncan (6:10): We've got crucems.
These three and others dance in front of 'it' (Mukesh 7:11) displaying their crossed fingers and taunting the chaser.
Alan: I've got crucems.
Duncan: You can only have crucems on the wall. You can't tig them off ground, because they've got crucems. If they haven't got crucems, you can tig them; that's how the game's played.
Mukesh tigs Duncan.
Mukesh: You're it.
Duncan: No, I had crucems.

Duncan is correct in believing that 'crucems' provides safety, but he fails to recognize that this word can be used independently of any other way of obtaining safety, such as jumping onto the wall. Nor does he know that 'crucems' allows you temporarily to opt out of a game for some legitimate reason such as 'tying up a shoelace', 'going to the toilet' or 'getting a drink of water'.

Identifying 'crucems' with safety is one step towards learning how to use it. Another would be to avoid being tigged by saying, 'I'm not playing', and drop out of the game, only to re-enter a few moments later with, 'Oh yes I am playing', as soon as someone else has been caught. This is a strategy popular with the youngest children, but there is nothing to stop them from invoking it whenever they are in danger and it is here that 'crucems' has an advantage. 'Crucems' is important because it restricts the reasons allowed for temporarily opting out and so does not threaten the break up of the game.

In other words, learning 'crucems' is not so much a great conceptual leap forward, but rather a little step down a path already well-trodden. And when we come to consider how preschool children solve the problems in which their older brothers and sisters would use 'bagsee', we shall see how verbal ritual is gradually prepared for in a number of subtle ways over the preceding years.

But having learned 'bagsee' and 'crucems' in First School, why are these rituals so little used in Middle School? In a sense, their power almost guarantees their demise, for children begin to turn these words back on themselves:

> *Lynn* (9:10):   Crucems.
> *Dottie* (9:6):   We're not having crucems.
> *Lynn*:   Bagsee-no-crucems.

Furthermore, as Jean Piaget pointed out, eight-year-olds are beginning to change their attitude towards rules. No longer are they seen as sacred and all powerful, but more as arbitrary conventions that can be changed, provided all agree. They are prepared to accept 'bagsees-not-allowed' before the start of a game and likewise 'crucems' may even be challenged in the middle of play:

> *Tim* (7:2):   I've got crucems.
> *Chris* (7:7):   There's no crucems allowed.

And when children finally learn the ultimate in verbal ritual of 'bagsee no bagsees', these words have lost much of their attraction, for as nine-year-old John explained, 'What you mean is that you can say bagsee the first time but not afterwards'.

PLAYING WITH WORDS

Ritual words have a well-established and clear meaning in the community. Other aspects of our actions, either what we do or say, may be more ambiguous. It is often the case that although we know what we intend, others interpret our actions differently. This can be both the cause of social problems as well as a way of solving them. Sometimes it is necessary to reassert the context within which an action is to be understood, while at other times it is this possibility of different interpretations that provides the solution. Although these various ways of playing with words are extremely subtle, they are not confined to adulthood. Children in the playground are equally adept in their use.

CLARIFYING THE MEANING

'Are you playing?', 'Is it a game?' It is important to find out, for actions such as hitting and wrestling can occur in either context. All that may be necessary is that one child repeats to the other the idea that 'it's play'.

> *Dylan* (5:1):   Let Batman shake hands.
> Dylan thumps Matthew.
> *Matthew* (5:3): You don't do it really.

> Neill and Pete are playing a skipping game.
> Neill (8:9) wraps a skipping rope round a little girl's neck.
> *Pete* (9:4):   Neill, we're playing skipping.

Of course, sometimes 'it's only a game' seems to have little to do with any previously playful activity, but appears to be an attempt to change an aggressive situation into a game and so avoid any unpleasant consequences.

> *Nick* (9:9) tells Tim who is holding Bob: You'd better leave him alone.
> Nick grabs Tim who lets Bob go.
> *Tim*: As soon as you've let go of me, I'll hurt him some more.
> Nick grabs Tim again.
> *Tim*: It's only a game, it's only a game.

Any such change of context might be resisted by explaining that what you intended was indeed far from pleasant.

> *Jamie* (7:7) to Matthew (6:8): Guess what Gary's done, he tried to get me round the neck.
> Matthew glares at Gary.
> *Gary* (7:6): I was trying to strangle him.
> *Matthew* to Gary: You're not playing.

Although there might be agreement as to the overall context or situation within which the actions are played out, there might still be confusion as to the implications for what is allowed at such times. For instance, sometimes the children agreed that they were playing a game, but disagreed as to the allocation of roles or turns.

> *John* (8:8): I'll have a go.
> *Pete* (9:5) and *Graeme* (9:3) You've got to wait your turn.

> *Malcolm* (6:0): I'm bionic, I'm bionic.
> *Gulan* (7:2) grabs hold of Malcolm and tells him:
> You're not bionic, you're not bionic.
> *Matthew* (5:3) is playing 'Spiderman' and tries to drag him
> away. No I'm not Spiderman, don't take me to gaol.

> *John* (8:3): What are you doing?
> *Neill* (8:6): I shot your legs, you were about to get a gun.
> *John*:   I wasn't, I'm on your side.

In these four episodes any disagreement was resolved by one
child asserting his own interpretation of what had been decided.
But at other times each participant might have quite contrary
views which they openly state.

> In a game of skipping:
> *Graeme* (9:3) to John (8:8) and Carol (7:9) We're both out.
> *John*: No, you're playing the wrong way, you're not playing
> right.

How can such conflicts be resolved? One way is to have a fight.

> *Malcolm* (6:10): I've got five chances.
> *Bob* (7:7): No, you don't have five chances in hopscotch.
> The two boys start fighting.

Another solution is to accept one participant's views, or failing
that, the aggrieved party can leave the scene.

> *Graeme* (8:10) to Pete (8:11) during a game of hopscotch:
> You're cheating, you chuck it on, you're meant to roll it on.
> *Pete*: You can do anything you like, chuck it, throw it.
> The boys continue to play according to Pete's interpretation
> of the rules.

> During a chasing game:
> *Neill* (8:9): You've got to run trackways, you can't do that,
> you can't turn back.
> *John* (8:3): That's your rules.
> *Neill*: He's not playing, he's breaking the rules. We were
> going to play until David spoiled the rules! We can't play,
> none of you can.
> *John* (to other boys): Let's go somewhere else.

CHANGING THE MEANING

All the episodes so far demonstrate how one individual can
clarify the meaning of his or her own and others' actions by
either restating the definition of the situation or by arguing
about the implications that each believes to stem from that
definition. Another way to solve problems is quite deliberately
to change the meaning of one's own or others' actions. I have
seen a number of ways in which this can be done. One method
is to redefine the situation and so place the action in a different
context. Another technique is to redefine the person who performed the action as in some way not responsible for what has
happened. While a third strategy is somehow to redefine the
act by, for instance, denying that it happened at all, or by
claiming that it is really more acceptable than we might think.

REDEFINING THE SITUATION

If you are approached by a nine-year-old who threatens to
'smash your face in', then it may pay to smile back and
graciously offer to 'let him off this time'.

> Ivan (9:7) grabs Graeme (9:3):
> *Ivan*: I'm going to smash your face in (and knees him in
> the stomach).
> *Graeme* does not react, then smiles and says: I'm going to
> let you off this time.

If Graeme had not turned this presumably real aggression into
a joke, but instead treated it as a real attack, then he would
have had to either fight or run away.
  The most striking instance of this strategy involved a group
of seven- and eight-year-olds who relentlessly attempted to
redefine a fight between two brothers, first as a game of
'mercy' and then as a wrestling match. When I saw this episode
I made careful notes, but it was some time before I came to
see it in the way I do now. It only dawned on me over the
following few months that this incident involved a highly
sophisticated solution. This is the difficulty with observing.
It requires both a certain amount of intuition to recognize an
important event when you see one, as well as a lot of patience
to let the patterns fall into place in their own good time.
  One lunchtime I saw two brothers fighting in a corner of the
First School playground. But whereas the younger, eight-year-
old Richard, was glaring and swinging his arms in earnest,
nine-year-old Nick had a smile on his face and was merely
defending himself against the blows. Very quickly a group of
eleven children gathered round and they tried to stop the fight.
One girl shouted, 'Cry mercy, Nick, cry mercy'. 'Mercy' is a
game that many of the junior girls play in which the children

interlock fingers, squeeze hard until one cries 'mercy', where-upon the other immediately releases her grip. Presumably this was an appeal to Nick to change the definition of the situation and hence the meaning of the action, in the belief that should he utter this magic word, Richard would immediately stop fighting. In the event Nick did not try this; perhaps he did not know about the rules of 'mercy', perhaps he had not heard the suggestion or perhaps he just chose to ignore it. When I later asked many of the children whether saying 'mercy' would stop a real fight, they all thought not, which means that the girl who made this suggestion still has some lessons to learn about the power of 'mercy'.

Within a minute the group started up a chant, with each child imitating the actions of a referee in a wrestling match. The count went from ONE right up to TWENTY-ONE before the two children disengaged. Was this because of or despite the chant? We cannot be sure, but it is clear that the spectators were attempting to redefine Richard's aggressive behaviour. In doing so, however, they were building upon Nick's own ambivalence. Even when the fight ended, I saw him run away fast and discuss with two other boys how much he disliked beating up his own brother.

So some seven- and eight-year-olds are aware that they can change the meaning of a playmate's actions by redefining the situation within which they occur. We have seen how they can turn someone else's aggressive behaviour into pretend fighting or a wrestling match. What happens, though, when they them-selves move between pretending and actually being aggressive? This turns out to be a extraordinarily powerful way of con-trolling others, for the recipient of such conflicting information has difficulty in predicting what will happen next and becomes distinctly uneasy. I know this because I have been on the receiving end. A friend pointed out my own unease during a playground encounter with a teacher who alternated between smiles and glares, so as to ensure that I would keep a promise to lend her school some lighting equipment. The true masters of this technique, however, were the boys at Middle School.

What impression does nine-year-old Ivan leave, when he rushes up and shouts, 'You asked for it now you stinking fucker', and then lets his face melt into a smile? Likewise, if you are grabbed round the neck and confronted with the ques-tion, 'Do you wanna fight?', what can you say other than 'No'? And it's just as well that your refusal would be quickly accepted with a playful, 'I'll let you off then'. These were typical of the ways boys at Middle School 'terrorize' each other. In all these episodes there is an incongruity between what a boy says and does, and this might be what is so powerful. Such examples are reminiscent of the archetypal gang leader or even teacher who maintains an aura of power by putting a knife to the neck of a comrade or pupil and laughingly sneers, 'I'm only playing'. It is perfectly clear just how easily he or she could change to being serious. Only rarely were either the verbal or non-verbal definitions of the situation challenged:

> *Ivan* grabs Ashok (9:6) round the neck and says:
> We're only playing, aren't we Ashok?
> *Ashok* refuses to accept this verbal definition of the situation
> and defiantly shouts: No.
> Ivan goes off.

DISTINGUISHING BETWEEN REAL AND PRETEND FIGHTS

The child who alternates between real and pretend obviously realizes the powerful effect of this sequence. He or she must also know what actions are appropriate under each definition. But this knowledge must be shared also by the other children, for should they fail to tell the two apart, the result would be constant misinterpretation and fighting.

How difficult a task is it for children to differentiate between pretend and real fighting? Among three- to five-year-olds the behaviour patterns are quite distinct. Observations by Peter Smith in Sheffield show that pretend fighting consists of smiling, running, jumping, hitting and wrestling, while aggressive behaviours such as pinching, biting, kicking, slapping, punching, throwing and grabbing occur at other times. When Sean Neill observed twelve-year-old boys, he found that their pretend and real fights are far less easily distinguishable.

Since we know that preschool children make a clear distinction between fantasy and non-fantasy, by saying for example, 'Let's pretend we're monsters', it seems likely that they can also distinguish between pretend and real fights. As the two are so obviously different, the task for them is much easier than for twelve-year-olds. If these older ones are also to avoid misunderstandings, then they must improve their ability to tell the two apart. Of course, there is an added bonus in becoming clear about the two situations, for since the two are behaviourally similar, there is now the possibility of changing from one definition to the other and in this way making one's actions difficult to interpret.

We still do not know exactly how children recognize pretend and real fights. Which features do they look for, or do they ask a bystander, 'Is this a real fight?' There are undoubtedly a certain number of children who fail to distinguish and react appropriately to rough and tumble (pretend) and real aggression. In First School I saw two non-English speaking children for whom this was a problem. Both these boys lashed out at others who continually touched them, misinterpreting these actions as aggressive rather than a friendly invitation to a chasing game. Happily, a sensitive teacher stepped in and successfully urged the others 'to be gentle' with the individuals concerned.

Distinguishing between real and pretend was even more of a problem for some teachers and the dinner-ladies. All these adults made the distinction, but emphasized how easy it was for an encounter to change its definition. They were often confused as to what was going on because of this.

First School Head Teacher: Teacher (Mr Morse):	Boys do enjoy pretend fighting, but very easily it can go over the edge to real fighting. It's part of playing and it looks as if nobody's getting hurt and then somebody comes yowling and obviously looks upset and then at that point you have to admit it's become real fighting.
First School Dinner-Lady (Mrs Jones):	Sometimes they have their little games and it would appear that they're fighting and I go up and say 'What's happening here?', and they say, 'Oh, it's all right, it's only play, we're not fighting'. And you just keep your eyes open to make sure it's playing, and invariably it is.
Middle School Dinner-Lady (Mrs Smith):	Well, if you do see them, and think they're fighting you go and say, 'no fighting'; and they say, 'it's all right, we're only playing', and I let them get on with it. You get to know which children (really) fight (a lot).

But one dinner-lady was so concerned about the possibility of pretend turning into real fighting, that she was unwilling to accept any 'horseplay' at all at playtime.

Dinner-Lady (Mrs Franklin):	They say 'we're playing' and then about five minutes later one of them comes to you crying and it finishes up like that; (though) you know it starts in fun. Well, you say (when pretend fighting starts), 'this will all end up in fighting if you don't stop'. They say, 'Ah well, we're only playing Miss', and in the end you sort of pull them apart from one another and say, 'if you don't put a stop to it, I'll fetch the Headmaster down'.

REDEFINING THE INDIVIDUAL

Whereas redefining the situation places any action in a different light, another strategy is to redefine the person responsible for the action and in this way discount what he or she does. In the following example it appears that Shweta coyly redefines herself as someone of tender years who cannot fully grasp the requirements of the game of hopscotch, and in so doing maintains her right to play as she pleases.

> *Caroline* (8:3) to Shweta (6:7): Hey, you're out.
> *Shweta* : It doesn't matter, we're only little.

What could Caroline say? 'No, you're not little, you're nearly seven' although possible seems unlikely. In the same way Graeme in the next episode redefines himself as momentarily incompetent at a crucial moment, in the hope of not having to suffer the usual consequences of his action.

> Graeme (9:3) takes a penalty kick but the football misses the goal. The other boys shout 'out', suggesting that he must temporarily drop out of the game.
> *Graeme*: Oh no, you were talking to me (when I kicked the ball).

Yet another way to redefine oneself is to deny agency. Indeed nothing can infuriate an adult more than the child who insists that 'it wasn't me', despite the inescapable evidence of our own eyes. Saying 'taxi' at First School is a ritual denial but often the denial is more improvised.

> Carol (7:9) physically attacks Jamie (7:2) after she has fallen over.
> *Jamie*: I ain't done it.
> *Carol*: Yes you did.
> *Jamie*: I never.
> *Philip* (6:10): It was him (and he points to Anthony).
> Carol attacks Anthony.

> *Gary* (7:6) falls over and says to Elena (6:7) Why did you do that?
> *Elena*: I didn't do that, I wasn't even talking to you.
> *Gary*: I'm going to get my mum.

REDEFINING THE ACT

If 'I didn't do it' is often difficult to believe, then 'it didn't happen at all' must be even harder to accept. Yet children are remarkably successful in their ability to deny all sorts of occurrences, particularly being caught in a chasing game.

> *Simon* (7:3) to Mukesh (7:11) in off-ground-tig: No you didn't touch me, you're cheating.
> Mukesh remains the chaser.

> *Alan* (5:4): This is den.
> *Adam* (5:10): I got you (tigged you).
> *Alan*: No, you haven't because you can't see me,

the gate's shut.

But you can't always get away with it.

> Gary (7:6) tigs Gulam (7:2).
> *Gulam*: You missed, you missed.
> *Gary*: No, I got you here (pointing to his arm).
> Gulam accepts the role of chaser.

Another less drastic way of redefining what has happened
is to give the actions a new label and so place them in either a
better or worse light. The precise description is all important
and in the examples below 'letting Ian go' becomes the more
acceptable 'he forced his way out', aggression is identified as
merely 'self-defence' and scoring a goal is relegated to 'showing
off.'

> *Lynn* (10:4): Why did you let Ian go? (Ian had been
> 'captured' by the girls).
> *Clare* (10:1): I never (deny act).
> *Lynn*: Why did you let Ian go?
> *Clare*: He forced his way out.

> Neill (9:2) hits Graeme (9:3)
> *Graeme*: Why did you do that?
> *Neill*: Self-defence.

> Neill (8:9) kicks the football and Pete (9:4), the goalkeeper,
> saves the shot. *Neill* claims about Pete: He's showing off now.

Finally, there is yet another way to redefine the act and this
does not involve relabelling but instead the assertion that what
we might believe to be to some extent morally wrong is really
the normal thing to do. Thus, among adults we might say, 'I
smuggled but everyone does it', and in the playground I heard
the following excuse for making a mistake.

> In a guessing game, *Neill* (9:3): It's on ITV at 7.45
> Fridays, beginning with P. [Nobody guesses.]
> *Neill*: Give up? ...Poldark.
> *Mary* (9:7): That's on BBC not ITV!
> *Neill*: You can't always be right, can you!

THE POWER OF WORDS

The impression that comes over again and again from examining
episodes of playground conflicts is just how powerful words
alone can be. A skilled mouth is an important asset and it
makes playtime predictable, for by and large children's
expectations are fulfilled. Some words such as 'bagsee',

'crucems', 'mercy' and 'taxi' have a clear meaning and are
rarely challenged. Other aspects of what children do or say
can be interpreted and re-interpreted to clarify or change the
meaning. What all the various techniques do is to make sure
that the unexpected does not happen. How do these strategies
fit together though? To find out, we must examine in detail
what happens during a number of everyday playground
problems.

5

'Whose game is it, can I play?'

Matthew (6:8): Can I play?
Gary (7:6):   It's my game, you can play, you're my friend.

When I asked the children if there were any problems at playtime,
most replied 'none'. Others complained about 'the bad weather',
'being tossed about', 'fights' and 'when your friends won't play
with you.' But every playtime there are many situations that,
although managed skilfully by most children, can cause problems
for others. Let us look at three of these – joining in a game,
obtaining or avoiding a role and being chased. Finally, I shall
describe what happens during fights.

HOW TO JOIN IN A GAME

The most basic problem in social life is how to join in the
activities of a group, and there are few children who do not at
some time or other seek out this opportunity. It was clear from
my own observations and what the children told me that there
are rules for what to do at such times. First, you must ask,
'Whose game is it?' in order to find out 'who's the boss'. This
is the child who 'started the game' and holds sole powers to
'choose the players and chuck out those who misbehave'. It is
to him or her that the request, 'Can I play?', or occasionally,
'Can I play, please?', must be directed.
    There are penalties for failing to follow the rules.
John (9:10) told me: 'If they say "I'm playing", not "Can I
play", then I'd swear at them and tell them to go away.' It is
times like this when a mistake is pointed out that provide an
opportunity to learn what is required.

    Jane to Helen: Can I play?
    Helen: It's not my game, it's Tracy's.
    Jane to Tracy: Can I play?
    Tracy: Yes.
    Jane: Do you want to play with Clare?
    Clare joins in.
    Helen: You've got to ask Tracy.
    Tracy: Yes (you can play).

Jane knows that she has to ask permission but seems to believe
that any participant can let her play. She is learning about the

45

special powers of the boss of the game and that her own inclusion does not confer ownership rights.

Whenever we speak of rules governing behaviour, it is tempting to believe that they must always apply. But this is rarely the case and although the rules were usually followed, they were not absolute. For instance, within an established group of friends it was not always necessary to seek permission. As one girl told me, 'You just go up and watch for a little while and they say, "Do you want to play?", and I say "Yes"'. Even rushing over and announcing 'we're playing' can be acceptable between friends, but it is not a suitable strategy for an outsider. A boy who imitated a group of girls with 'I'm playing' was pathetically left ignored, even though he jumped up and down waving his hand in the air.

As for other methods, I once saw inclusion achieved through the successful use of 'bagsee can I play?', and on another occasion a group of nine- and ten-year-old girls turned to the democratic procedure of voting to decide the issue. When confronted with, 'Can I play?', some of them put their hands in the air and shouted, 'I vote yes'. Since there was no dissenting voice, inclusion was achieved.

The only child who consistently joined in games without seeking permission was Neill, who achieved this in the First School where he was known by his peers as 'the boss of the playground'. But on starting Middle School, he too abided by the rules.

Following the rules, however, does not automatically let you join in. The way you ask the question is only one condition for entry, the other being that your presence is desired by the boss of the game. What happens when inclusion to a game is denied and how does the excluded child cope? There are a variety of strategies available.

HOW IS EXCLUSION ACHIEVED?

Exclusion may be achieved by merely saying 'No', 'No, I'm sorry', 'See you' or 'Get lost', but quite often children revealed their reasons for exclusion. And these excuses give some hints as to what is valued in the playground world.

Friendship is important and lack of it can be grounds for exclusion:

Tim (7:2) to Bob (7:7): I don't like you, go away.
Chris (6:9): I'm not playing with you, I'm playing with my friend.
Of course, being friends facilitates inclusion:
Matthew (6:8): Can I play?
Gary (7:6): It's my game, you can play Matty, you're my friend.

The fact that by and large the sexes play separately (less than 20 per cent of total interactions in First and Middle Schools were cross-sex) may also be used to justify exclusion.

Ramesh (8:8): Can I play?
Annie (8:9): No, boys can't play.
Ramesh goes off.

Boys and girls of this age usually prefer companions of the same sex and if this were not the case, then 'boys can't play' would carry little weight. Conversely, it is precisely because children from Indian families do play with white companions that I have never seen anyone excluded from an activity with the phrase, 'Indians can't play'. Such an injunction would only have any social force were the playground as racially divided, as it is sexually.

As we have seen there is some advantage to 'owning a game', since it is this child who can 'make all the suggestions, choose who can play and chuck people out if they don't behave.' Exclusion may be backed up by 'it's my game' or alternatively, saying 'it's someone else's game' shifts the onerous decision onto another player.

Fiona (9:3): Can I play?
Beckie (9:6): It's someone else's game.
Rowenie (9:6): No you can't, I'm sorry, 'cos we're getting too big (a group).
Fiona goes off.

This last exclusion was not challenged presumably because everyone knows the value of having a small group. Similarly, children are generally reluctant to admit others when a game is already in progress and exclusion may be claimed on these grounds alone.

Neill (8:9): You can't play, we're in the middle of a game.
An argument follows and eventually both boys present their cases to the dinner-lady.
Neill: We're in the middle of a game.
Pete (9:4): You can't stop me.
The dinner-lady tells them to play together 'nicely' and they follow her advice.

But being in the middle of a game does not automatically provide grounds for exclusion, for some games have rules that specify how to include another child at such a stage in the proceedings. In 'grandmother's footsteps' and 'May I?' the convention is that all the participants have to go back to the starting line. But I saw one eager participant suggest that this rule be waived and was happy to accept a disadvantage in exchange for easy inclusion.

How do children exclude others? They can try appealing to
their ownership of the game, to a lack of friendship, that it's
a boys' or a girls' game, that the group's too big or that the
game's already in progress. And eight-year-old Pete told me
about another strategy:

> I say, you can't play and if you do join in, I'll tell Miss
> that someone's interfering with our game.

COPING WITH EXCLUSION

What strategies are available to counter exclusion? Many children accept it and just 'go away' or 'start up their own game.'

> *Gary* (7:6): Hey you're not playing, it's my game.
> *Malcolm* (7:4): Come on let's get the girls.
> Gary and Malcolm run off together.

Others may accept exclusion but try to extract some sort of
punishment. In the next episode the offender suffers the penalty of losing some of his play equipment, what might be called
the 'I'll-take-my-bat-and-wickets-home' solution.

> *Dylan* (6:4): You're not playing.
> *Lynne* (5:7): That's my skipping rope.
> Dylan gives her the rope and she goes off.

Quite often children tried to reverse the decision. They told
me that 'you keep on asking' and say 'please'. Or you might
'ask someone who's playing to persuade the boss' or even
threaten that 'next time it's my game, I won't let you play.'
   The opposite to a threat is a bribe and it too is a powerful
tool. Anthony (6:9) told me he promises others to 'let them
come to his house', but more often bribery involved sweets,
since these are both a desired and scarce commodity in the
playground.

> *Malcolm* (7:9) to Damad (7:6): You're not playing.
> Damad produces a sweet.
> *Malcolm*: It's my game, I'll let you play, (and he points to
> Damad). He's it.
> Damad gives all the players sweets.

It is worth noting that in this exchange Malcolm not only
gained a sweet, but he also avoided being 'it' by giving this
role to the child who wanted to play. The price of inclusion
may be even more clearly stated:

> *Vimala* (6:0) to Clare (6:4): You've got to give her some
> crisps if you want to play.

But even bribery is not always successful:
Neill (9:2): Let's play, Javed?
Javed (9:5): No.
Neill: I'll give you a sweet.
Javed: Let's see (and he looks at it for some moments
before replying) No.
Neill walks off.

Another possibility is to treat the exclusion as some sort of
mistake and it may only be necessary to point out that you have
the required permission.

In a skipping game, *Pete* (9:4) Get out Carol ...
Carol (7:9): Mary says I can have her place.
The boys let her take part.

Even more subtle is for the excluded child to rule the
exclusion out of order, by claiming that 'we're playing another
game.' But alas the boy in the next episode who tried this
strategy was ignored.

Gary (7:6): It's ip dip, you're not playing,
you're not playing, it's my game.
Mitch (7:6): No, we're playing another game.
Gary takes part in Mitch's game whilst still 'denouncing' it.
None of the participants pay any attention to Gary and
eventually he says to Mitch: OK then, you can play.

Powerful though words and sweets may be, disrupting the
game may at times be even more effective. When refused a game
of football by a group of nine-year-olds, a group of twelve-
year-old boys took the ball away and since none of the younger
ones dared retrieve it, the older ones were eventually allowed
to join in. Similarly, many of the older boys told me that they
would 'beat 'em up' to gain inclusion, but the only child I saw
continually to use this tactic, and incidently fail with it, was
nine-year-old Nick.

Nick: Hey Matty, can I play?
Matty: No.
Nick: I'll beat you up.
Chris: You leave him alone.
Nick goes off.

Nick joins in a game of football without permission.
The players tell him they do not want him to play and add,
'Fuck off'. Nick attacks them, takes the ball away, throws
it far away down the playground and then walks off.

Nick to boys playing football: Let's play?
Tim: No.

Nick: Go on.
Tim: No.
Nick starts to kick a player.
Tim: Now you're certainly not playing.

How do children cope with exclusion? They might accept it
and go away or start up another game. To try and reverse the
decision I saw children claim that they already had permission,
bribe the other players or disrupt the game by taking away some
of their equipment or beating up the participants. In addition
they might complain to the adults present, for it is one of their
principal goals that 'children should all play together nicely.'
Though perfectly understandable, it inevitably brings them into
conflict with the children themselves, for whom a certain amount
of exclusion is daily practice.

WHICH CHILDREN ARE EXCLUDED?

Although it is clear that there are rules for joining in a game and
a variety of methods to achieve or counter exclusion, most
teachers, parents and dinner-ladies would want to know why it
is that some children come to be excluded and not others. As
yet this issue has not been studied in detail, but it does seem
that some children such as Nick do not follow the rules for
joining in and have not developed adequate strategies to cope
with the ensuing exclusion. How can these children best be
helped? Should we be teaching them the appropriate skills?
They certainly do present a problem to the dinner-ladies on
duty and they reported mixed success with their attempts to
help.

Mrs Jones: We say, 'Come on and all be good friends and play
together' and it usually works.
Mrs Franklin: They play with them for a little while but
then they get tired and they're back on their own again.
Mrs Smith: Well we can't really do anything about it,
because if there's children who won't play with them, you
can't force them to play.

HOW TO OBTAIN OR AVOID A ROLE

Having been accepted as a participant in an activity, a child's
problems do not immediately cease for there are other hurdles
to be jumped. The group has to decide what to play and since
many games offer a number of different roles, there may
be some competition as the children strive to obtain or
avoid them.

APPORTIONING ROLES AT THE START OF A GAME

In Chapter 3 I discussed the variety of methods available to
choose a player for a particular role, but I said little about
the problems that can occur when children actually use these
techniques. But among the infants there were few disputes, for
roles were invariably apportioned 'in a flash', with a child
either accepting a role, 'You be "it"', or occasionally by volunteering themselves, 'I'll be Batman'.

I only twice saw these five- and six-year-olds use dips and
in the episode below they ran into problems, for this group of
youngsters was clearly unwilling to consider the outcome as
binding. Although they started to choose 'it' with the dip 'ip
dip dog shit, who's "it", not you', they eventually gave up and
resorted to pinning this role on the last to arrive.

> Jamie counted out and Anthony was chosen to be 'it'. He
> objected loudly, 'No, I'm not "it"'. Jamie reluctantly agreed
> and repeated the dip but alas once again Anthony was the
> loser. Just as he raised afresh his complaint, Jamie saw
> Anthony's cousin Philip approaching. Turning towards the
> new arrival he shouted, 'Philip can be "it"'. Unfortunately,
> Philip, like his cousin, was far from keen on the idea. The
> ensuing argument only ceased when all three boys trium-
> phantly screamed at Nicholas as he arrived on the scene, 'He's
> "it"', and so the game commenced.

The seven- and eight-year-olds also chose 'it' in a flash
('let's play tig, Simon's "it"'), but in addition they used a wide
variety of ritual methods. These included turning round and
quickly saying 'bagsee-not-it', races such as 'the last one to
the wall's "it"' and of course the use of counting out or dipping.

None of these methods guarantees against problems. When four
nine-year-old girls all shouted 'bagsee-not-it' in unison, one of
them gallantly solved the problem by volunteering, 'Oh, I'll be
"it".' Another group of girls all shouted, 'me me me' on being
asked by one of their peers, 'Who wants to be "it"?' The power
to make a choice was then given to the retiring 'it'. Races that
result in a draw also demand a solution. When this happened
between two nine-year-old girls, they quickly and secretly
decided who should be yellow and red, and then asked the
outgoing 'it', 'Yellow or red?' The one whose colour was chosen
became 'it'.

DIPPING

Dipping provides ample opportunity to avoid being 'it'. One
group of children that I observed had so many conflicts over
alleged cheating that I thought it would be interesting to film
them. Every day for a week they spent half-an-hour out of

class with me and each time they started and finished with the
dip, 'Racing car number nine'. They seemed completely
unperturbed by the camera. Here is an extract from one of the
ten sessions that I filmed.

> During the dip, Mukesh (5:9) has to say a number.
> *Arthur* (8:8): Say a number straight away.
> *Ramesh* (8:8): Look at my finger. (He puts up one finger.)
> (Ramesh and Mukesh are brothers.)
> *Malcolm* (7:9): Don't you dare say one.
> *Ramesh*: Look at my finger, say a number.
> *Mukesh*: Four.
> *Malcolm*: That's not fair, you counted that.
> Ramesh, Malcolm, Arthur each have one foot left in; Mukesh
> none. The count lands on Arthur.
> *Malcolm*: You're not allowed to count.
> *Arthur*: You're going to start (the count) with you (Malcolm)?
> *Malcolm*: Don't you dare say three.
> *Arthur*: Nine.
> *Malcolm*: You cheat, you cheat, you cheat by thinking.
> *Arthur*: I did not.

Arthur's crime was that he could count ahead, even when the
other boys placed their hands over his eyes. He also knew that
his predictions depend upon where the count starts from and
so he often stipulated the foot on which it should begin. He
was often challenged and frequently suffered hands being
placed over his eyes. But he successfully rebuffed these challenges by claiming, 'I didn't (cheat), he was over my eyes,
how could I count?' He sometimes even explained the basis for
his success, 'I thought he had two (feet left in), he had one
and he had one' and the fact this his admissions were ignored
suggests that the others did not realize that it is possible to
count with one's eyes closed. No wonder they claimed, 'You
cheat by thinking'. And he could even afford to go along with
their complaints and replace his foot, only to 'cheat' again.
   The other boys, Malcolm, Ramesh and Mukesh also 'cheated'
but in different ways. Malcolm managed to avoid ever being
'it' partly because he was always the one who did the counting
and partly through working out what number to say, should
the dip land on him. Being the dipper meant that he could
skip over syllables or miss out feet and choose either to ignore
or pursue any complaints. No one ever put their hands over
his eyes, which was just as well because he easily got confused,
and had to think carefully about which foot to start counting
on. At such times Arthur might correct him, particularly if he
had already been counted out himself.
   When Ramesh had to say a number, his little brother Mukesh
benefited more often than he did. Indeed, on one occasion he
even changed his number specifically so that Mukesh could
withdraw a foot from the circle. When it was Mukesh's turn,

Ramesh held up a certain number of fingers and the chances
were about even, both that the little brother would accept the
advice and that the advice would help him. On the other hand
Mukesh was not totally ignorant of what was happening. Although
his command of spoken English was very poor indeed (the family
had only recently come from Bangladesh), he once intervened
to tell Ramesh, 'I told you to say two, crazy' and demonstrated
how two would count Ramesh out.

TRANSFERRING ROLES DURING A GAME

In many games invidious roles are passed on by being caught.
Often merely running fast can help avoid this fate or saying
magic words such as 'crucems' or 'I'm not playing'. Even more
effective is to venture only rarely out of a safe area and so gain
permanent immunity. But this may be challenged as 'not fair'.

In off-ground tig, Mary (9:2) jumps a short distance
from the safety of the railings.
Beckie (9:6): You've got to run out (further);
it's not fair if you don't run out.

These solutions fairly clearly fall within the rules, but a child
might be even cleverer with words and try to redefine what has
happened, either by denying being tigged or by claiming 'I
got you back.'
In off-ground tig:

Gary (7:6) tigs Gulam (7:2).
Gulam: You missed, you missed.
Gary: No, I got you here (and he points to his arm).
Gulam goes off and tigs someone else who turns round
and says, 'I'm not playing.'

Threatening to exclude another player who dares accuse you
of being 'it' is another strategy and one that was fairly commonly
employed.

Jamie (7:7): Gary's 'it', Gary's 'it'.
Gary (7:6): It's ip dip.
Gary to Matty (6:8): You're not playing, because it's ip dip.
You have to put your leg in to see who's 'it'.
You're not playing, you're not playing,
It's my game, you've got to do ip dip.

In the face of these ways of avoiding being 'it', I have seen
the chaser either become frustrated and try physically to drag
a child from a safe position or use the more subtle tactic of
trying to involve another person on whom to divest the 'it'
role. This is fine if the other player is willing to join in, but as

we shall see this strategy may be unsuccessful if the new
player is an unwilling observer or even an inanimate object.
'The wall's it' just will not do.
   In tig-off-ground.

> *Beckie* (9:6): cannot tig anyone so she tigs the observer,
> Andy, Andy, you're 'it' (involve another player).
> Observer looks away and does not respond.
> *Beckie*: Oh, I'll be 'it'.

   In tig-off-ground.

> *Gary* (7:6): No, I'm not 'it', you're still 'it'.
> I'm not playing (claim immunity). I'm not 'it',
> I got you back (redefine act).
> Damad, shut up, you're 'it'.
> *Damad* (7:6): You're 'it'.
> *Gary*: You're 'it'.
> *Gary* to Matty (6:2): You get him down.
> Matty pushes David off the logs (physical violence),
> and David tigs Matty who is not playing (involve
> another child).
> *Gary*: Matty's 'it' and he chases Matty shouting,
> 'Tig, tig, off-ground-tig'.
> *Matty* accepts the invitation to play but asks,
> 'Tig means you go like that doesn't it?' and he
> swings his arm through the air.
> *Gary*: Matty's 'it', Matty's 'it'.
> *Damad*: Matty's 'it'.
> Matty cannot manage to tig anyone so he touches
> the wall: The wall's 'it', the wall's 'it'.
> *Damad and Gary*: No, you're 'it'.
> Matty goes off.
> Mickie is passing.
> *Gary and Damad*: Mickie's 'it' (involve another child).

There is more to 'the wall's it' than we might immediately
think. Mistakes like this are crucial for understanding the
complexity of social life, for it is only when something goes
wrong that we can understand why it usually 'goes right'. 'The
wall's it' illustrates the problem of formulating an acceptable
solution to the problem of being unable to tig another child.
This ability rests upon understanding the implications for what
is allowed that stem from the definition of the situation. It is
clear that Matty was unsure of what 'Matty's "it"' entailed; he
knew that tigging involved waving his arms in the air but
not it seems that he necessarily had to touch another person
in preference to the inanimate wall. No wonder he left the
scene, but perhaps episodes such as this one provide the
contexts for learning about the nature of many situations and
what sorts of actions are allowed in each.

HOW TO BE CHASED

Merely repeating a child's name over and over again may be all
that is necessary to cause him or her to chase you. In addition,
the name may be followed by 'try and catch me' or a more
provocative utterance like, 'Brad's "it", the big fat shit', or
'Brad, Brad, he's mad, he's mad.' 'Brian's getting eggy,
Brian's getting eggy' was another one that I heard, where
'eggy' is a word used in the Oxford area which means that
someone is getting angry and about to launch an attack. Pete
(8:11) told me about a similar phrase, 'He just can't take it
any more', meaning that 'he doesn't like people going on at him.'
On another occasion I heard the chant of Jan (6:4) and Wendy
(6:0), 'You can't catch us, you can't catch us.' It worked,
for Elizabeth (7:8) quickly replied, 'Yes I can catch you' and
set out after them.

The next episode demonstrates a number of ways in which to
get someone to chase you.

Five girls Chris (6:8), Jenny (8:9), Mary (7:0),
Sheila (9:1), Alison (7:6) to Duncan (7:6):
'Cheese face, cheese face.'
Jenny: Chase us.
Duncan: I'm not going to chase you.
The girls: Duncan, Duncan, dirty face.
Chris: White hair, Duncan is a dirty face, old granny
faddock. (Duncan does have very blond hair.)
All the girls poke at him. Duncan hides behind a nearby wall,
then reveals his presence and starts to chase them. On
catching Chris, the two pretend to fight and disengage.
Chris; 'Old granny faddock', and swipes at him with a
paper hanky.
The girls shout: The boys are getting eggy, the boys
are getting eggy.
Chris: Duncan, Duncan, Duncan.
Duncan goes off, Alison follows him, he turns round to say,
'Not playing'. He tells the girls, 'I don't want Alison to
play, I don't need her to play.'
Chris: Only Joy can play, he only wants Joy.
Jenny: Do you want Clare?
Duncan: Clare - yeah.
The girls use their toilets as a safe retreat and try
to get Duncan to chase them.
Duncan: I'm not playing, go on clear off.
Playtime ends.

This episode incorporates many of the aspects already mentioned. In order to try to get Duncan to chase them, the girls
reel off a list of nicknames all concerning aspects of his person -
they claim he's getting 'eggy', got white hair, a dirty face and
call him 'old granny faddock'. These have the required effect,

but Duncan proves to be quite aware of the power that he has
in the game, threatens withdrawal (I'm not playing) and dictates
which girls are allowed to tease him.
    It seems that to be chased one can merely demand 'chase us',
but it may be more effective also to offer some 'low-level' insult.
The children told me the following nicknames: piggy, conker-
brain, faggot, skunk, twit, blackjack and scaredeycat, which
would all do the trick, as well as more provocative statements
such as 'telling lies about them by saying they're in love.'
Some of the older boys were even more direct in their provoca-
tion and suggested you should 'push 'em or kick 'em'. But let's
remember that not all children want to be chased. When I asked
eight-year-old Teresa, 'How do you get someone to chase you?'
she paused, looked at me incredulously and replied emphatically,
'But I don't want anyone to chase me!'

HOW DO FIGHTS START?

During my many months of observing at playtime, I only saw
twenty-two fights and many of these I arrived at when they were
already quite literally in full swing. Only on five occasions was
I there to see the start and these showed what might be
expected - that children can come to blows for a variety of
reasons: disagreement over whether a goal has been scored in
football, arguments over the rules of hopscotch, retaliation for
exclusion from a game or after being called a racist nickname.
    Just like a teacher or dinner-lady, who arrives on the scene
after all the action is over, it is possible to ask the children
why a fight started. But often they too were unsure or were
unwilling to commit themselves. One nine-year-old boy told me,
'I don't know why he wanted to fight, but he wanted a fight
so I gave him one'.

HOW DO FIGHTS PROCEED?

(a) *The role of the crowd*
When a fight started in the Middle School playground, a crowd
almost instantaneously arrived. Although First School children
were also willing spectators, the pulling power of a Middle
School fight was far greater, and they much more actively
encouraged the participants to fight on:

> Two nine-year-old boys from Asian families are fighting and
> about fifty other children, mainly older boys, gather round.
> The crowd chants, 'Oxford Aggro, Oxford Aggro',
> and then 'Paki aggro, Paki aggro'. Eventually a teacher
> breaks up the fight.

Usually the crowd split into two factions, each supporting its champion:

> Fight between two nine-year-old boys, Javed and Nick.
> *Javed* to a spectator: Sacha, can you stop it?
> He's fighting me.
> Sacha makes no reaction.
> *Spectator 1*: Go on Nick.
> *Spectator 2*: Go on, Javed, smash his head in.

Such encouragement from the crowd to stand firm must make it difficult to back out of a conflict. A child who does so may be chastised in no uncertain terms to return to the action:

> Are you a chicken?
> Are you scared to fight?
> Just go up to him, hit him in the knees,
> that's all you have to do.

(b) *Speech between contestants*

Whilst fighting, children often exchanged insults. They shouted, 'You sod', 'Get lost' or 'Fuck off', and addressed each other by surnames and nicknames such as 'twinkletoes' or 'fatso' and even spat at each other. At times they also asked each other questions and these referred to the concept of a 'fair' fight. To ask, 'Why do you always pick on me?', suggests that there are rules as to who can be attacked. I recall a Middle School boy who told me in the playground, 'You're lucky you wear glasses, 'cos we don't hit kids with glasses.' The next episode reveals that fights are only thought to be fair if they are between equals, either in age or build.

> Nick (9:9) grabs hold of a boy and starts
> fighting; it seems that the act is unprovoked.
> Two other boys shout: leave him, leave him, pick
> on someone your own age, coward.
> *Bob*: How old are you?
> *Nick* lies: Eight.
> *Bob*: You have to pick somebody smaller than yourself
> (don't you). Leave him, leave my friend.
> Nick lets go.

HOW DO FIGHTS STOP?

When I put this question to the children, the majority told me that 'Miss' or a 'dinner-lady' intervenes. Only four children (all at First School) referred to the idea that children might sort out the conflict for themselves, by 'giving up', 'stopping when they want to', 'stopping when someone gets hurt' or by 'making up with each other'. Observation, however, revealed many more ways in which fights can terminate; not only 'Miss' intervened, but the other children did as well. Sometimes they physically broke up the fight, sometimes they threatened the combatants with the power of an adult, ('His mum's coming') and sometimes they treated the real aggression as if it were pretend and in this way brought the fight to a close. In the last chapter, I gave an example of this last tactic - the crowd tried to turn Nick and Richard's fight first into a game of 'mercy' and then into a wrestling match. In another episode a spectator tried the same strategy with the same children and it worked. Annis went right into the middle of the mêlée and offered a sweet to her brother Richard who was fighting. She seemed to bring about a change in his attitude for he looked up, smiled and changed his real fighting into pretend.

On this occasion Richard had taken up his brother's battle, for nine-year-old Nick had started the fight by kicking Mike who retaliated with 'I'll tell my mum on you.' On another occasion when Nick and Mike fought, the other children physically intervened.

In First School, during a game of football,
Mike (8:6) shouts: 'I scored'.
Nick (9:4) the goalkeeper makes no reaction,
so Mike gives him a little kick.
All the other children say in unison,
'Uuuuuuuuuhhhhhh' (the pitch of the voice rises and then falls), Mike and Nick pause for a moment when they hear this sound and then engage in full physical contact, fighting for the ball.
The other children quickly break up the fight by physically separating the two boys.

What is the significance of this long drawn out 'Uuuuuuuuuuhhhhhh'? I heard it only in the First School and it seems to signal that some crime has been committed, with possibly an added note that trouble is brewing. The children could only tell me that 'it's when somebody's done something wrong.'

Intervention may involve much more than just pulling two boys away from one another. In the next episode, the child who intervenes offers John the opportunity to join in another group's activity. This is arbitration at its best.

Fight between John (9:1) and Henry (9:11).
Henry: You're not going to pick a fight with me,
I told you.
John still attacks with some boys watching.
Another boy now physically separates the two.
John is crying.
The Intervener talks to both boys and asks John: 'Do you want to play with us?' and John goes off with him.

Finally, let's look at the following encounter that traces the whole course of a fight and includes many of the features that I have just mentioned. As happened so often during seven-year-olds' games of football, the fight started because the boys disagreed whether a goal had been scored. One child claimed he had been picked on, a crowd gathered, there were accusations of name calling and finally the incident ended with the excuse, '(I didn't mean to kick you), I was aiming at the ball.'

Mike (8:6) shoots the ball into the goal drawn on the wall.
Nick(9:4): Hit the post, hit the post.
Nick should give up his role as goalkeeper but doesn't.
Neill (9:1), Pete (9:4), John (8:4) and Mike all try to wrestle the ball off Nick.
Pete accuses Nick: You don't pick on anyone else, do you?
John: Nick, come on.
Neill: Pete, Pete. (A crowd gathers and the children take sides.)
Pete to John: I thought you said you wouldn't call me names any more.
John: I didn't say I wouldn't.
Pete: As you came across you kicked me.
John: No I didn't, I kicked the ball.
The excuse is accepted and the fight stops. The boys continue their game of football.

CONCLUSIONS

By examining how particular problems can be solved, we can see how the solutions that I outlined in the previous chapter come into play.One way to avoid a role is to use the ritual words 'bagsee-not-it'; another is to redefine the act of being tigged as 'you missed'. One way temporarily to opt out of a game is to say 'crucems'; another is to shout 'I'm not playing' and so redefine yourself from a participant to a bystander. One possible way to stop a fight is to cry 'mercy', another is to treat it as if it were a wrestling match. But not all solutions use verbal ritual or the ways of playing words that I have already mentioned.

In some situations there are rules for how to proceed. Such is the case for joining in a game. Save in exceptional circumstances, the inquiry 'Can I play?' must be directed to the 'boss' of the game whose role confers the power to exclude others at will, by saying, 'It's my game.'

Other justifications for exclusion such as 'You're not my friend', 'Boys can't play', 'We're getting too big a group' and 'We're in the middle of a game' alerted me to another type of solution. I asked myself why it was that these justifications for exclusion were not readily questioned; why children only rarely asked, 'Why can't boys play?', or asserted 'The group's

never too big', or 'So what if I'm not your friend'. It seems
that these excuses work because they refer to shared goals in
the playground community and ones that are relatively difficult
to challenge; in this case that the sexes should play separately,
that there should not be too many people playing a game and
that you should only play with your friends.

Similarly, some of the other methods which the children used
to get their own way also rest upon commonly held goals. Should
an individual threaten another with loss of friendship then this
would probably have the required effect, for it is a reasonable
assumption that all children desire friends. Threatening
exclusion so as to avoid a role with, 'You're not playing',
presumes that all children want to participate in group activities.
Bribery with sweets so as to reverse a decision to exclude might
work because children for the most part desire food. More
generally, being able to do as one pleases may be threatened
by the well-known power of adults, or more directly by other
children's physical violence. Why did being called 'white hair'
and 'old granny faddock' cause Malcolm to chase the girls?
Perhaps he felt that his image was being threatened. Likewise,
boys cannot easily walk out of a fight without putting their
reputation at risk.

Many of these strategies that rest on children's presumption
about their playmates' goals in the playground are ways of
threatening others and they work because they add some new
meaning to the action. The threatened child is informed how
the threatener will perceive the action should it occur and,
in particular, what consequences are to be expected.

In the next chapter I shall examine what children aim to do
at playtime and the coping strategies that arise out of knowing
one another's goals.

6

'I'm your friend, let me have some'

Jamie (5:0) approaches Jim (5:2)
who is eating his morning tuck. He puts his palm
out and demands, 'I'm your friend, let me have some.'
Jim hands him a crisp.

Five-year-old Jamie's method of obtaining food from Jim was to
turn the situation into an implicit test of friendship. Jamie
presumed that Jim preferred to share some of his crisps rather
than lose a friend. There are many other solutions of this type,
ones where knowledge of another person's goals provides a
strategy to get them to do as you want.

But how easy is it for one child to realize another's goals?
There are two possibilities. The simplest way is to assume that
someone else's goals are exactly the same as your own. Three-
year-olds typically make this assumption and quite often they
are correct. As they grow older, however, children begin to
develop what might be called true social empathy. They learn
to anticipate what another person might think or feel, precisely
when these thoughts and feelings are different from their own.
It is the development of this ability to infer someone else's
goals from either what they tell you, or from what you see them
do or say, that occupies much of childhood.

Although it is undoubtedly true that some children have
highly individual goals at playtime, I want first to examine
those goals, which were by and large shared by the whole
community. For example, all children wanted at some time or
other to join in a group, to eat sweets and to gain friends.
Knowing this enabled them to threaten each other. Another
type of threat was to invoke the sceptre of adult power and I
often heard references to various kinds of grown-ups and their
potential to make the children's lives a misery.

There are also more personal goals. Like adults, children need
to maintain self-esteem (a positive view of themselves), and
this partly depends upon the way others come to see them - in
other words their reputation. Threatening another child's self-
esteem or reputation is a powerful source of control and this is
why nicknames, especially racist ones, or claims such as
'you're in love' are so effective. We shall come to these later.

PARTICIPATION IN A GAME

There can be little doubt that for most children participation in
a game is at some time or other eagerly sought after. There are
two ways in which this knowledge offers strategies of control.
A child may threaten to exclude another player with 'you're
not playing', and so manage to avoid an unwanted role. Alternatively threatening one's own withdrawal from an activity with
'I'm not playing' may also be perceived as a threat. Its effect
lies in the possibility that if the group break up, each member
is now faced with a new problem, that of either being alone or
of trying to join in another group's activities. It's not surprising that 'I'm not playing' may well be resisted.

> *Dylan* (6:0) tells Jim (6:1) the rules of a pretend episode:
> If you escape, I'll set your clothes on fire.
> *Jim*: No, I'm not playing, (threatens to withdraw).
> *Dylan* grabs him by the chest: You are playing,
> you are playing, (threat returned).
> The role play continues.

FOOD

Food, and especially sweets, are always welcome in the playground. Their value arises from their scarcity due to the
closed nature of the school, where children are not usually
allowed out to buy sweets at lunch time, even if they have the
money to do so. Thus an interest in sweets is rife:

> *Martin* to Jake: Hey I know someone who'll give you a sweet.
> *Jake*: Who.
> *Martin*: Delia.
> *Jake*: Oy, Delia, let me have a sweet.
> *Delia*: No.

Since sweets are valued they can be used towards goals.
Children of all ages told me how they can achieve entry into a
game or be used to barter.

> *Mukesh* (7:11) to Dylan (7:3): Can I borrow your football
> boots please? I'll give you two little sweets and two
> big ones.

FRIENDSHIP

Everyone would agree that just as participation in an activity
is sought after by most children, so too are friends. We have
already seen that threatening loss of friendship can be used to
obtain sweets, but what sorts of friendships do children have

in the playground? Many of the teachers told me that companions come and go and friendships are merely temporary associations. But my own observations of who was with whom at playtime show that the children had clear preferences to be with partic- ular playmates. Nevertheless, explicit mention of friendship was often used as a tool and this could easily have misled the teachers into believing that here was a community of constantly changing companions.

Josh (8:2): Can I have the gun? I'll be your friend.
Mukesh (5:9): Give me that hat back, I'm your friend.

Bridget (9:3): Let's do handstands.
Beckie (9:6): I don't want to do it.
Bridget: I'm not your friend; ... you can't.
Beckie: Yes I can.

Philip (6:9) asks Matthew (6:8): Can he (Johnnie) play?
While Matthew thinks, *Philip* adds: Go on, be a friend.
Matthew lets Johnnie join in.

Friends to Philip are not just temporary partners and the next episode shows how potent a timely reminder of friendship can be.

Philip (6:9) is knocked over by Anthony (6:9)
and Jamie (7:2) picks him up.
Philip looks very annoyed and is about to beat up
Anthony. *Jamie* restrains him on the ground and
repeatedly tells him in a soft voice:
'He's your friend really; isn't he, isn't he?'
Eventually Philip nods agreement and now that he
has calmed down, Jamie lets him go.

HOW ARE FRIENDS MADE?

Whenever a new child enters a school he or she needs to quickly make new friends. The Opies describe a ritual that does just this, though I have not observed it myself: 'Children link the little fingers of their right hands and shake them up and down declaring,

Make friends, make friends,
Never, never break friends.

They quarrel and their friendship is ended with the formula.

Break friends, break friends,
Never, never make friends.'

Few children in my schools could recall how they made friends, but one boy told me about a ritual handshake to seal the friendship:

> *Pete* (8:11): Once I tried to be friends with Jamie
> and he pushed me over into a big puddle and I got up
> and started chasing him and we shook on it, to make
> sure that we're friends.

One solution to the problem of making new friends is that of
adoption. Even in the nursery, older girls often take younger
ones under their wing, but the most striking episode I saw
comes from Middle School. On arrival at her new school, nine-
year-old Vimala was so much in demand that arguments raged
between jealous second-year girls competing to be her guardian.

> *Lynn* presents Vimala (9:2) to Cheryl.
> *Lynn* to Vimala: Do you like her?
> *Lynn* tries to get Vimala and Cheryl to shake hands.
> *Vimala*: I'm her friend, I know I'm her friend.
> She refuses to shake hands (i.e. it's not necessary).
> *Lynn* to Vimala: We were the first to find you and we
> have to look after you.

> *Sunita* (9:6) to Vimala (9:2): Who do you love,
> us lot or Maria?
> *Vimala*: I love everybody.
> *Sunita*: But you don't even play with us though.
> *Vimala*: I will play with you, but I want Maria
> to play with you (too).
> *Sunita*: But she plays sissy games, she plays mermaids.

THREATENING WITH THE POWER OF ADULTS

One of the strategies that children frequently employ towards
goals is to invoke the power of adults. Children are well aware
that their freedom of action is limited to what the teachers and
dinner-ladies will allow. I was told that the dinner-ladies, 'walk
round and stop fights', 'tell people off if they're naughty',
'make sure that no one gets hurt' and 'keep guard on us to
make sure that we do everything what we're meant to.'
   The ladies themselves confirmed the children's perceptions:
'We are someone for them to talk to and if anything goes wrong
they come to you.' 'We generally watch the children and try to
sort out their problems, like when they have all their little
squabbles', and intervene they certainly did. In Middle School
they mainly just stopped fights without being concerned with
why they had started, but First School children actively took
their disputes to them and demanded arbitration. At such times
the dinner-ladies usually held on-the-spot inquiries, calling
'named' children to give evidence and usually ending up with
an appeal, 'not to be so silly' or to 'go and play together

nicely'.

Taking disputes to arbitration is one way to use adult power, but the mere threat to do so may be all that is necessary.

Ramesh (8:8) picks up the football.
Adrian (5:10) shouts: You're not allowed to
— kick it.
Jim puts his arm up in the air: I'm telling
Miss, I'm telling Miss.
Jim goes off to find a teacher and Ramesh
drops the football even before any adult
arrives on the scene.

Rather more surprising were those occasions when I heard children threaten one another with the dreaded 'mum'. Can such a threat be successful? Just as the child who is told 'I'm telling Miss' must believe that the teacher or dinner-lady is likely to intervene and fears the outcome of such arbitration, the child who threatens his playmate with 'I'll tell my mum' must provide similar evidence, and of course the mother's arrival on the scene is far from likely, unless she happens to be a member of the school staff. On one occasion, however, this type of threat did work.

In a game of football Mike (8:6) takes the ball
from Ben (8:1).
Ben: Don't you.
Mike pushes Ben who walks away.
Mike: Twinkletoes.
Ben stops for a moment then chases Mike.
Mike: Twinkletoes.
Ben punches Mike in the back.
John (8:8) says to Ben: Leave him alone,
his mum's coming in a minute.
Ben stops fighting.

THREATS TO SELF-ESTEEM AND REPUTATION: NICKNAMES

It is usual practice among children to address each other by the first name and most alternatives to this seem to be disliked. Although a few girls told me that they welcomed certain names such as 'pussycat', 'Raquel Welch' or 'tea strainer' ('because of my freckles'), for most children nicknaming can cause distress. For instance, Jan (6:4) and Wendy (6:0) reduced their older friend Debbie (8:7) to tears by continually calling her 'Debbie the Pebbie'. Yet somehow or other, children have to learn to cope with such insults.

Philip (6:9) to teacher: Miss, Miss, they keep
calling me names.

Jamie (7:7): Sticks and stones may break your
bones, but names will never hurt you.
Teacher: Don't call him names.
Jamie: We're teasing him, Philip's a little
spoilsport.

Contrary to the rhyme, names do hurt and this traditional
saying offers both some protection against them as well as
ensuring that the practice continues. One of the functions of
nicknames is to push somebody into an action by insulting them,
but if the aim is only to start a friendly chase then the insult
should not be too great. It would be interesting to find out
just which nicknames are acceptable and which call for physical
retaliation. The girls in a previous episode, who taunted
Duncan into chasing them with 'cheese face', 'dirty face', 'white
hair' and 'old granny faddock', were certainly aware what was
the appropriate level of insult.

Hints as to which nicknames go too far in another culture
come from a friend of mine, Bill Delay. He reports the nicknames
in use at his old school in Sri Lanka during the 1930s. They
referred mostly to the food generally eaten by an ethnic group.
Sinhalese boys had to suffer being called 'jak seed fellows' or
'rice gruel fellows'. Ceylon Tamils were appropriately called
'palmyra nut fellows', because the palmyra palm is about the
only tree that grows well in Jaffna where most of the Tamils
live. Indian Tamils, on the other hand, were called 'dhal fellows',
because dhal or lentils were a major item of their diet. Although
somewhat derogatory, these nicknames were not considered
objectionable. Caste or religious differences were not referred
to, because they would be taken as personal insults, which
would call for some form of physical retaliation. In the case of
the Moslem boys, however, reference was made to the fact that
they were circumcised, and they were called 'tip-cut-off-
fellows'.

I heard a number of nicknames in the playgrounds: some
rhymed with the real name, some referred to a child's physical
appearance (pig, fatso, four eyes) and others pointed to an
aspect of character (twit, scaredeycat, puff, chicken). But
before leaving this subject, I want to mention two further types
of naming – address by the surname and racist names.

ADDRESS BY THE SURNAME

An important distinction in playground life is between calling
your peers by their first names or their surnames. It seems
that just as in adult society, the use of surnames or both names
together has the effect of asserting your own authority.

During a tussle over property,
George (8:9) to Sussanah (9:0): Stop it, stop it.

Anne (7:9) to Sussanah: Look here fatso.
George: Sussanah Price.

In a game of football,
George (8:9); Best is a kicker, Best is a fouler.
Anne (7:9): Four eyes (the well-known nickname for a
child who wears spectacles).

Where do young children learn the power of this form of
address? We just don't know. It would be tempting to believe
that they copy it from their teachers, but in this First School
as in others the children were always called by their first name.
Address by the surname is more typical of Middle and Upper
Schools. But the element of social control is only clear if there
are also times when first names are used. I vividly recall a
teacher from my own schooldays, who one day informed our
class that he now called his eleven-year-old pupils by their
first names. He told us that in breaking with tradition, he had
also discovered that whenever he wished to exercise any
authority, he could revert to calling them by their surnames.
I was surprised by his amazement, for this was a fact of which
we pupils were only too well aware.

RACIST NAMING

One physical attribute that has particular significance in our
society is skin colour, and I occasionally heard children being
called 'black face', as well as other racist names. We can be
sure that children from minority racial groups do not like to be
addressed in this way and these names cannot help but give a
certain amount of respectability to racist ways of describing
others. In the next episode, Malcolm and Gary called Damad
'brown boy, brown boy' to push him into chasing them, but
this nickname goes too far and Damad attacks them. The
exchange is especially interesting since it also includes many of
the other strategies that I have discussed – denying responsibility for an act with 'I didn't do that', threatening to 'get
my mum', threatening 'I'm not playing', appealing to the
observer to intervene, asking the aggressor to stop fighting
and finally, complaining to the teacher on playground duty.

Malcolm (7:9) approaches Gary (7:6): Hey, are you called
Garth or Gary?
Gary: Gary.
Malcolm: Let's go after them.
Malcolm and *Gary* jump up and down shouting: Brown boy,
brown boy.
Damad (8:2) chases them, catches them and they start
pretend fighting.
Elena: (6:7) to Malcolm and Gary: You don't call

my friend that.
Gary falls over (or is pushed) and says to Elena: Why did
you do that?
Elena: I didn't do that, I wasn't even talking to you.
Gary: I'm going to get my mum.
He goes off.
Damad and Malcolm are fighting.
Malcolm: I'm not playing, I'm not playing.
Damad still does not release his grip.
Malcolm: Andy, Andy (observer) get him off.
I want you to get off me. Look, leave off, will
you. Will you stop messing about.
Damad releases him and Malcolm complains to the teacher
on playground duty 'they're after me'.
She ignores him.

THE ABILITIES BEHIND RACIST NAMING

Invoking racist nicknames, although distasteful, is not without
skill. For correct usage, children have to be aware of their own
and others' racial identity, and it is now clear that even three-
to five-year-olds can make this distinction. They also need to
realize that racist names have a restricted use to annoy a
member of a specific racial group. The next two examples show
that some young children are not aware of this second distinction and use the nicknames regardless of racial membership.

Kate (7:2) calls Sara (7;0) (both white): 'nig-nog, nig-nog,
nig-nog.' Sara does not react.

Philip and Anthony (both from Asian families) are fighting.
Anthony (6:9) to Philip (6:9): 'Pakibasher'.
Jamie (white 7:6) to Philip: 'Pakibasher', and after a
tussle all three end up talking together.

Whether or not a child suffers from racist nicknames, the
task of having to come to terms with being a member of a
minority racial group is by no means easy. The boy in the next
episode clearly has problems in this respect.

Mukesh (7:11): I know who your mother is.
Fiona (white 8:7): You don't know who my mother is.
Mukesh: She's got black hair and a brown face.
He runs off.
Fiona: He's talking about his own mother. I don't understand
this.
She chases after Mukesh and tells him: That wasn't my
mother's face, whoever said it, ignore it.
Mukesh runs off and shouts at Mickie (white 8:2): Black
face, black face.

Mickie chases after Mukesh.

Despite evidence, such as the previous episode, that some
children had difficulty adjusting to being different, racism was
not rife in the two school playgrounds where I observed.
Children at times called each other racist names, but it seems
that at least the younger ones were unaware that these epithets
were anything more than just 'ordinary' insults. The problem
is that the namers do come to learn about the specifically racist
aspects of these names, as do the named. Furthermore, their
use remains, partly because these insults have by now already
become an everyday aspect of playground life.

However, children who are discriminated against are not
totally helpless. On one occasion I saw a white boy refuse to
kiss a girl from an Indian family during a game of 'postman's
knock.' One of the white girls supported him, but the four
others threatened to walk out, if the racist had his way. They
lectured him on the different, but equal races throughout the
world, and when he still wouldn't change his mind they came
out on strike.

MAINTAINING A REPUTATION: 'NOT BEING SEEN WITH THE OPPOSITE SEX'

We have already seen that 'boys can't play' is a powerful way
for girls to exclude boys from a game. It seems that one of the
values of the playground community is that almost by tradition
the sexes do not play together. Yet a substantial minority of
cross-sex interactions were observed; between 15 and 20
per cent.

This shared belief that boys and girls ought to play apart
seems to be maintained by a certain amount of teasing between
the sexes, which publicly affirms their animosity. Sometimes
the boys disrupted a girls' game by joining in without permission, or vice versa the girls disrupted the boys' games by
getting in the way. One group of twelve-year-old girls, each
at least 5'8" tall, used their superior height to unfair advantage
and destroyed a game of football. They took away the ball from
the smaller nine-year-olds and threw it to each other, way above
the little boys' heads.

At other times, there was more interaction between the sexes.
Children at both schools played 'boys onto girls' or 'girls onto
boys'; a game which consists of a chase followed by a certain
amount of teasing of the prisoners. Typically the girls used
their toilets as a safe area for escape, and then teased the boys
who stood at the door ready to pounce and occasionally dragged
the weakest ones inside. Once I saw the reverse, when an
eleven-year-old boy took refuge in the boys' toilets from the
same group of tall girls whose continual torment was to
threaten to kiss him.

The following episode includes typical insults between the
sexes.
Mary (9:2) captures Neill (9:3) and shouts,
'Sit, sit'.
Neill: No.
Mary: We'll pull your ears.
Neill doesn't sit.
Mary: Sit ,.. We'll take your trousers and shorts down.
Mary to another girl: Go on, get him (get Ashok).
Neill to Ashok: Go on, (run away), they're after you ....
Ashok (to observer): Andy help.
Mary hits Neill saying: You've got to watch out.
Neill: Ashok can run faster than me.
The girls catch *Ashok*, who shouts at them: Knickers.
Neill: Shut up Ashok.
Mary: I don't wear knickers, I wear pants.
Ashok: You've got a boyfriend, haven't you.

Some of these insults can be taken out of the context of
teasing and used by themselves during arguments.

Neill (8:4): Be careful Bonehead.
Mike (8:3): Neill, your girlfriend's Ginny.
The two boys spit at each other.

It is clear that to be seen to have a boy- or girl-friend is
not desirable. One eight-year-old girl teased her male playmate
with, 'Football players don't have girlfriends', but it appears
that even in First School they do. Eight-year-old Pete told me
about the difficulty of managing these relationships.

Author: What do you teach the infants?
Pete: We don't teach them our secret games that we like
            the best. Me, Neill, John and Mike, we play with the
            girls a lot and they like to play 'kiss-chase' with us,
            and they get all their girls and they start chasing
            us and chasing us and chasing us and they catch
            everyone else and kiss them all. And they all have
            to go out, then it's me versus about twenty girls,
            'cos I'm always in the front. There was once, there
            was ten girls at one end and ten girls at the other
            blocking the entrances. I come zooming round the
            corner smash straight through the wall.
Author: Why do you have secret games?
Pete: Because if we tell anyone else they'll all start teasing
            us and that.
Author: Why do they tease you?
Pete: They'll say we've got girl-friends and we play with
            the girls.
Author: Is it not very good to have a girl-friend?
Pete: Well it's all right if you can keep it a secret for

quite a long time until someone finds out, then they start telling everyone else and bang goes your secret.

Author: Why does it have to be kept a secret?

Pete: I don't know. It was Neill's idea to keep it a secret, but he's not here today.

Author: Does he have a girl-friend?

Pete: I don't know her name.

Author: Does she come to school here?

Pete: No.

Author: Do you have one?

Pete: Yes.

Author: Is she at school here?

Pete: (silence) I haven't told anyone about my girl-friends; I've got loads of love letters at home.

Author: Do other boys have girl-friends?

Pete: Most of the boys in the school have got a girl-friend.

Author: How do the new children learn about the secret games?

Pete: By the old people who leave; they leave their secrets with the new ones. Me and Neill always meet our girl-friends in the little playground down the bottom of the alley. Me and Neill don't approve of meeting our girl-friends in the big playground where everyone can see.

Not only do other children disapprove of emotional attachments, but so did one of the First School dinner-ladies.

Mrs Jones: They had a spell of kissing games, you know, trying to kiss one another, but we soon scotched that.
Why?
Well we just thought of it as a bit silly, and not hygienic really, spreading the germs about and things like that. I believe we mentioned it to the Head, but anyway we just told them and it died a natural death.

GAINING A REPUTATION

Much of what we do or say is primarily intended to show others what sort of person we are; this is how we gain a reputation. In any community certain actions earn respect and in my playgrounds boys seemed to be far more concerned about how others saw them than were girls. What contributes to a boy's reputation? While watching at First School, I began to realize that the ability to win races was greatly admired, while at Middle School, it seemed that they were concerned to be seen to be tough. There must be many other reasons, however, why one child comes to command the others' respect.

REFLECTED GLORY OF ONE'S FATHER

Some children are admired, not for their own actions, but
because of the reputation of their fathers. Since the dads are
not present to confirm just what they can and cannot do, their
offspring are happy to vouch for them.

Among a group of ten-year-old girls,
Lynn: My dad weighs 11 stone.
Cheryl: My dad weighs 13 stone.
Bridget: My dad weighs 16 stone.
Anne: My dad weighs only 9 stone.

The First School Head Teacher told me of her involvement in
the following argument among nine-year-olds.

Mukesh complains to Head: Andrew says that his dad
can beat up my dad.
Andrew: Tim says that his dad can beat up my dad.
Tim: We were discussing whose dad could beat up
whose dad.
Head: Mukesh, have you ever seen your dad beat up
anybody? Does he go around beating people up?
Mukesh: (shame-faced) No.
The other boys answer likewise.
Head: You shouldn't offer that your dad will beat up
anybody, if you know that they'd never do it.

WINNING RACES AT FIRST SCHOOL

The seven- and eight-year-olds, particularly the boys, were
always eager to race and found every opportunity to do so.
Being let out of class, for instance, could easily become a race
to the playground:

Malcolm (7:7) announced: I'm the first junior to
touch the playground.
Fiona following close behind adds: I'm the second
junior to touch the playground.

Malcolm was always keen to be first, and on another occasion I
heard him offer Dottie the following challenges in quick
succession.

Last one to the bench is a looney!
First one to touch the bench is smart!
First one to touch the logs is the greatest!
First one to touch yellow!
Dottie objected: You're near to it!
He replied: First one to touch white!

An intense interest in races seems to be fairly typical of this age group. A friend of mine recalls similar experiences at his old Primary School. At the end of each term the boys always organized their own completely unofficial races, which consisted of about thirty laps round the playground and occasional sprints. Apparently 'race-fever' did not grip all the children, but a good many boys eagerly practised for the big day. The main difference that I noticed in Middle School was that the races were rarely held for their own sake, so as to establish the fastest individual, but were instead incorporated into more complicated team games, of which racing was merely one aspect.

BEING SEEN TO BE TOUGH

When the nine-year-old boys came up from First to Middle School, they received plenty of advice about how to stick up for themselves. Fairly typical was a twelve-year-old's criticism of a nine-year-old, who had just run away from a fight:

Are you a chicken? Are you scared to fight? Just go up to him, kick him in the knees, that's all you have to do.

In general, the older boys seemed to 'test out' the newly arrived first years.

David (12) pushes Graeme (9:8) and he falls over.
David: You're weak, you're weak.
Graeme: So what.

Graeme was determined not to be 'put down', either by David or by anyone else.

Sam (12): Hey you (Graeme) Smith, if you run over there to that wall and come back within ten seconds, I'll give you 5p.
Graeme: I want to see you do it first.
Sam: You do it, then I'll do it.
Graeme walks off.

For some boys, however, being at Middle School meant that they could now threaten that an older brother would come and beat up anyone who annoyed them. But this ploy brought with it the risk of being called a 'chicken'.

Nick: I'll get my brother (onto you).
Tim: You're a chicken.
Bob: I'm going to beat your brother up.
Nick attacks Bob.

'Chickens' were confined to the Middle School playground and this was a powerful insult. For instance, when Neill heard Louise shout across the school yard, 'Neill is a "chicken"' he felt bound to reply, 'Anyone can bash up Louise', he said 'just one little punch and she's down'. Although there were no 'chickens' at First School, there were 'scaredeycats', and I was one of them. When a nine-year-old girl turned a skipping rope round and round in front of my eyes, I blinked and she shouted 'scaredeycat'. This insult does not have the same force, however, as 'chicken', which accuses you of being scared of your peers.

The most obvious pointer to the importance attached to being seen to be tough was the sheer frequency of discussions about fighting.

Graeme (9:8) discussing with a group of ten boys:
Terry: Can you beat your brother up?
Graeme: I gave him a black eye.
On another occasion;
Jude: Did you get beaten up by Morris?
Did he beat you up easily?
Graeme nods.

Along with all this talk about fighting, there was also the appearance of episodes in which boys tested out each other's toughness. What was striking was the extent to which insults and accusations flew about, but there was never any real aggression. Nearly always, the episodes ended with both boys smiling.

Tony grabs Ashok by the neck and holds him down:
'You're a chicken, you're a chicken.'
Ashok: No I'm not ... Fatso, fatso are you a chicken?
Tony: No, I'm not. He smiles and lets go.

Garth: I could clip you into the gutter.
Ben: No, you couldn't.
Garth: Do you want me to punch you in the guts?
The two boys tussle and Garth gets Ben into an arm twist.
Garth: Say sorry, say sorry.
The bell calls an end to playtime and the two boys laugh and smile at each other as they go into class.

The goals that I have described in this chapter are ones that are generally shared by the whole community. But of course no two children are exactly alike, and if we are to understand what children learn at playtime, then we must first find out what each individual does there. The next chapter is the story of one particularly interesting individual and his career as 'boss' of the playground.

7

'Neill's the boss of the playground'

During a race Neill and Ginny finish at the same moment.
Neill: Yes, yes (I'm the winner).
Ginny: Draw.
Neill: No, it wasn't, you're just trying to
make trouble.

So far I have described the many different tactics that children employ in a variety of conflict situations. I have not had much to say about individuals, yet we all know that no two children are exactly the same. They have different needs, get into different problems and solve them in their own characteristic manner.

I first began to think about this question of individual differences when I noticed that one boy in the First School playground was particularly successful in getting his own way, despite doing so by frequently breaking what I took to be the rules of the community. This boy, Neill, was known by his peers as the 'boss' of the playground and I was able to observe him both in First and in Middle School. Since he was so often involved in conflicts, I obtained a good deal of data on him.

Of the ten children that I watched over a period of two years, as they went from First to Middle School, Neill appeared in about 40 per cent of all the problem episodes that I recorded. In addition, I spent two weeks at the end of Neill's first year at Middle School solely observing what he did at playtime. During this period I was so well known by him and his group of friends, that I joined in their daily games of football and thus became a participant observer. But before putting my impressions, I want to look first at what is known about children's different styles of interaction.

INTERACTION STYLES

Much of our knowledge about individual children's goals and strategies in social interaction comes from two impressive observational studies, both of which started around 1970. One is by my colleague, Margaret Manning, in Edinburgh, while the other comes from Hubert Montagner and his team in Besançon, France.

There are as many individual styles as there are children. How many we choose to lump together and call a group depend on the particular aims of the research. Hubert Montagner wanted to 'discover the manner in which communication develops at a time when language has not yet appeared.' He filmed children aged between seven and thirty-six months in a crèche and three- to six-year-olds in a Nursery School and comments about how their interaction styles endure through to the Primary School.

Margaret Manning's investigation centred on a narrower theme - is it possible to classify three- to five-year-olds according to their dominant style of hostility, and if so, do the groups share other characteristics? She observed seventeen children over their last year and a half at Nursery School and watched them again four years later in their Primary School playgrounds when they were eight.

Despite their rather different goals, both Montagner and Manning independently identify ways of interacting that are remarkably similar. We start by looking at the behaviour profiles that Montagner noted.

MONTAGNER'S STYLES OF INTERACTING

Leaders

As their name suggests, the leaders are the best-adjusted children. In the crèche Montagner describes them as being friendly and appeasing, in ways that are appropriate to the situation. For instance, they often greet their friends at the door when they arrive in the morning and rush to console them should they burst into tears or be about to cry. All this causes others to approach, and imitate them, and they are frequently offered objects.

Their attractive manner even extends to conflicts, when rather than seize objects, threaten or fight, they are similarly friendly, and in this way manage to avoid further aggression. When the leaders are themselves threatening, they express it most often through a sequence of non-ambiguous gestures, which are neither preceded nor accompanied by aggression. Indeed, they usually wait for a reply to their threat before hitting out. But generally a leader would only be as aggressive as was strictly necessary to obtain the desired goal, the victim usually turning away, standing aside or abandoning the object without complaint.

They show much the same pattern at Nursery School. There are frequent friendly and appeasing acts but their threats are now shorter and less distinct. These are often reduced to pushing out the chest, raising the arms, furrowing the forehead, all accompanied by what Montagner coyly refers to as 'naughty words'.

The leaders are the ones who organize activities in the classroom and playground, create new games, play with objects in an original way and are used by the teachers to organize others. All in all, they can be considered to be the best adapted to the changing rhythms of life and to interchanges with others. They move easily between home and school, have many diverse ways of communicating and are easily understood both by children and by adults. 65 per cent of Montagner's leaders showed the same style of communication at the crèche, the Nursery School and the Primary School. In only 15 per cent of cases did leaders at three become more fluctuating or more aggressive in their behaviour at four. These changes coincided with modification in the family environment between the third and fourth year.

It is worth mentioning in passing a group of children who resemble leaders in being friendly and rarely aggressive, but who are not so successful in competitive situations. Compared to the leaders in Nursery School, these ones are twice as often displaced from a location, and similarly unsuccessful in obtaining a desired object. They are less attractive than leaders, being followed and imitated by fewer children, but because they are nevertheless friendly, they do not become isolated.

Dominant-aggressive
Some children in the crèche are frequently aggressive both in free play as well as in competitive situations. Their aggression seems to be spontaneous and not as a response to any threat. Sometimes the aggression alternates with isolation, and the greater the frequency of the aggression, so the duration of the isolation increases. These children are not at all responsive to their peers. For instance, when they make a threat they do not wait for the victim's reply, but pass straight to aggression, and they rarely initiate any friendly overtures. Even when they are friendly, their sequences are often interrupted without any clear reason. 'In other words, dominant-aggressive children, perceived by their peers as turbulent and aggressive, can at any moment, express a succession of disordered gestures and gratuitous violence.'

At Nursery School the profiles of these children remain basically the same, though the frequency of their aggression diminishes considerably between three and five years. However, they are still very brusque and disorganized in their movements and frequently disrupt others' activities. It is not surprising that teachers come to label them as naughty'.

Although other children often avoid their presence, they are at times followed and imitated, especially during noisy games, such as 'cops and robbers' or 'cowboys', which often take place in the playground. Their well-developed gestures and very noticeable activities are potentially very inviting, but should any conflict arise, then their aggressive side quickly shows itself. This causes them to be abandoned and rejected by others, which in turn brings further aggression, and isolation.

They show the same style at Primary School, though Montagner suggests that the presence of teachers in the playground leads them to simulate aggression with pretend blows rather than resort to real fighting. Their aggression shows itself in

starting scraps by interrupting or disorganizing games and
they are sometimes so violent as to cause injury. Even more
than in Nursery School, they can give the illusion of being
leaders, but in reality they are not the leaders they claim to
be. They do not have the same power to draw away others and
are abandoned by many of their followers. With their reputation
for naughtiness, they tend to use aggression and isolation as
ways of replying to adults who, not surprisingly, threaten and
reject them.
  Lastly, Montagner noticed some children who fluctuate, either
daily or weekly, between being a leader and being dominant-
aggressive. He notes that they usually stay fluctuating up to
three years and then either become more unstable and tend
towards the style of dominant-aggressive or stabilize towards
the profile of a leader. The way it goes, he claims, depends on
the nature of any changes within the family.

Dominated children
Certain children only rarely assert themselves in competitive
situations. However, within this dominated group, there are
still differences in behaviour profiles. I have already mentioned
the dominated ones who resemble leaders and Montagner points
to three other styles: dominated-aggressive, timid-dominated
and totally withdrawn children.

Dominated-aggressive These children are rather like the
dominant-aggressive ones. Their behaviour is not organized
into sequences and teachers watch out for them being isolated
and aggressive. They change little between three and eight,
though the frequency of their friendly exchanges tends to
increase, while their aggression diminishes. Their hostility still
arises for no obvious reason and alternates with long periods of
isolation, often between fifteen and thirty minutes.

Timid-dominated Some children in the crèche are particularly
fearful and withdraw from their peers at the slightest provoca-
tion. However, after a prolonged period of isolation they often
go in for bouts of very violent aggression, comparable in its
nastiness to dominant-aggressive children. Despite the fact that
they offer and appease like leaders, they still suffer the most
hostility. In addition, these children constantly solicit the
teachers' attention and are thus very demanding.
  They are much the same at four and five, though their fear,
withdrawal and flight are now both less marked and less frequent. If they are at all jostled, threatened, upset or attacked,
they nearly always burst into tears and just as before they can
suddenly come out of their isolation and be extremely aggressive. These children find it very difficult to accept any new
structures, like, for instance, changing school. They take two
to three months to settle in, but once accepted into a group,
they too can give the illusion of being leaders. When a conflict

or competition develops or they are attacked or repulsed, then they quickly take on their true profile.

Withdrawn Montagner has little to say about the few children who are totally withdrawn in the crèche. At four or five some are still like that; they seem without any goal, lean against a tree or wall, or just curl up on the ground. Should others try to interact with them, they fail to reply and isolate themselves even further. Even when they are older, they can spend the whole of the playtime without ever being seen to give or receive any solicitation.

MANNING'S STYLES OF HOSTILITY

Specific specialists

These children mainly practise what Manning has called specific hostility - manipulative hostility aimed at settling a dispute about property, precedence, roles or rules, etc. They use hostility only in situations which frustrate or annoy them, as a tool to get their own way, and the victim is often incidental. Most of them show little aggression and very little violence. They are outgoing, self-assertive and friendly and often become popular leaders of the Nursery Class.

Harassment specialists or teasers

Other children specialize in harassment - unprovoked, 'out-of-the-blue' teasing. These ones are among the most hostile and violent children in the Nursery. They are less friendly and less popular and often wander from table to table in the classroom disrupting activities. At times these children are imitated and followed, but they get very angry when opposed, and this leads to them being rejected and abandoned by their peers.

Manning noticed two types of teasers. Some show a lot of initiative and are good at attracting other children to them. However, their games rarely last long because they fail to allow the other participants any scope. These children resemble Montagner's dominant-aggressive group. Other teasers are more like his dominated-aggressive ones; they tend to be withdrawn and for long periods do not interact at all. They do not appear to enjoy their isolation - these are not children who are happily absorbed in a task.

Manning suggests that these various characteristics of teasers can best be understood if we see them as intent on proving to the world and to themselves that they can be someone, that they can do things of importance that have an effect on people. The outgoing ones, in particular, want to be the boss, to dictate the rules and to say how things should be. They like to be the leader and so play games in which they can exercise their power over others, such as Batman, Tarzan, witches or ghosts. The more withdrawn ones just seem to bear a 'grudge' against other

children. Although some specific specialists share the aspira-
tions of the outgoing teasers, with them it is tempered by the
desire to be liked, to co-operate and to be friendly. 'To my
mind teasers in general are so abnormally "hung-up" with a
need to assert themselves that more normal attitudes go by the
board.'

Games specialists

Manning identified a third group of children who are normally
friendly but who go in for bouts of very violent aggression
during games. These ones also spend a lot of time seeking the
teacher's attention, demanding help, complaining when in
difficulties and tending to make a great fuss when hurt. Their
approaches to other children are also strange, sometimes
teasing, and often displaying or boasting. Although normally
little trouble, these children have periods of wild excitement,
usually in a game of some sort, when they appear to become
'out-of-control', and almost invariably manage to hurt someone.
One four-year-old, for instance, found that when he was a
robber, there was one little girl who was particularly frightened
by his frequent invasions of the Wendy house. She always
cowered into a corner and screamed. Soon he took to singling
her out and became even more frightening and intimidating on
each successive robbery. Eventually she had to be rescued by
a teacher.

These children, obviously, need to be the centre of attraction.
They find that the easiest ways of attracting attention are to
tease, to display as a monster, to splash water and so on. They
do not seem to notice that they are actually hurting their friends.
Manning suggests that because they give so much of their
thought to attracting others to them, they less often do things
which would in fact make them interesting and enable them to
achieve their goal.

The extent to which Montagner and Manning's observations
complement each other is remarkable. Manning's specific specialists are equivalent to a combination of Montagner's leaders and
the ones he saw who are dominated but nevertheless resemble
leaders. Manning's teasers are a combination of Montagner's
dominant- and dominated-aggressive children, and her games
specialists resemble Montagner's timid-dominated group. A
point by point comparison reveals no major points of disagreement between the two researchers.

I shall follow Manning in distinguishing just three styles which
I shall call leaders, teasers and attention seekers. Although the
distinctions arise from observations of two- to five-year-olds,
they are still useful for describing the interactions of older
children. In discussing Neill's personality between the ages
of seven and nine, they help us to decide whether he really
was the leader that he claimed to be.

NEILL

At First School
What sort of person was Neill at First School? In our talks
together Neill told me a bit, but not a great deal, about his life
in the playground. Most of my conclusions come from examining
playtime conversations in which Neill himself participated, as
well as ones which referred to him.

Neill was one of the most popular boys in his class. He was
frequently the centre of attention at playtime. But over and
above his popularity was his reputation of being the 'boss' of
the playground. Recall that the 'boss' of a game has the power
'to make all the suggestions, choose who can play and chuck
out those people who misbehave', but Neill's power went much
further than that. Many of the children complained to me that
they could do nothing about his cheating 'because when you tig
him in "British bulldog", he says he's in the air when he isn't',
having earlier evoked the 'bagsee no tigging in the air' convention. Similarly, he always managed to join in games of football
without first seeking permission to play, and this was in contrast to every other football player. To cap it all, he was the
only child who frequently attempted to ignore the power of
'bagsee'.

> In football:
> *John* (8:8): Bagsee goal.
> *Neill* (8:9) has the ball and says:
> I'm in goal, (and stays there).

On this occasion he overturned the power of 'bagsee', but I
once saw his own use of 'bagsee' challenged. Perhaps this was
because he had gone against the conventional use of 'bagsee'
as prefacing a request and instead tagged it on at the end.
Nevertheless, he still retained an element of control, for he
managed to nominate a third party to the coveted role.

> *Neill* (8:9): I'm in goal, 'bagsee'.
> *Nick* (9:4): No, I'm in goal.
> *Neill*: No. John's in goal.
> John goes in goal.

Neill's opinion was extraordinarily influential, and his
interpretation of the meaning of an action would invariably
stick.

> *Graeme* (9:3) kicks the football and it hits Neill and
> goes into the goal.
> *Neill*: It hit my hand last.
> *Pete* (9:4): It still counts, doesn't it?
> *Neill*: No, it doesn't.
> *Arthur* (8:8): The one who scores goes in goal.

Neill stays in goal.

But I did once see Neill lose an argument. One of his favourite techniques was used against him – another child threatened that she would withdraw from the game and he fell into line.

> In 'roll over' there are two teams of children and each team makes a cordon by joining hands. When a child's name is called he or she runs across and tries to break through the cordon. A successful child goes back to the team from which the run commenced, an unsuccessful one joins the new team.
> 'Roll over, roll over, let Joy come over.'
> *Neill* (8:9) to Joy (9:0) who are in the same team:
> You've got to run as fast as you can.
> Joy doesn't manage to get through the arms of the other line.
> *Neill*: Cheat, cheat, cheat, she's got to go back.
> (To Helen, of the other team) You made her go slow, (redefine the individual).
> *Ginny* (9:0) (on Neill's side): She slowed down, she wants to be on your side.
> *Helen*: She didn't go through, she tried to go through. I'm not playing if we don't have Joy (threat to withdraw).
> *Neill*: Don't play.
> *Helen*: I won't then.
> *Ginny*: Joy, come on, no cheating.
> (To Mary and Helen on other side), They're cheating, aren't they? Yes, they are.
> The game continues and Joy stays on Helen's side.
> Helen's threat to withdraw from the game was effective.

These episodes make it clear that Neill was respected as 'boss' and was frequently able to get his own way in the playground. But was he a 'true' leader? When we look closer at what he said and did, it becomes clear that he was, to some extent at least, 'hung up' about being the 'boss' and intolerant of any opposition. These characteristics resemble much more the children that Montagner and Manning describe as teasers. These children are intent to prove both to themselves and to others that they can be someone. With Neill, this particularly showed itself during races.

Winning races
Neill took winning races very seriously, but he had the problem that since he was not the fleetest of foot, success rarely came naturally. Once when he was in the lead, he looked round over his shoulder and, spying that he was a good few yards ahead, ostentatiously danced the last few yards home singing, 'Boys and girls come out to play'. His showing off was presumably

meant to give the impression that for him winning was easy, but it was not, and the very last thing he would ever admit to was that he had lost.

> Carol (7:9) is being timed as she runs round a course in the playground.
> *The children* watching shout: She's going to win, she's going to win (and so beat Neill who had been timed earlier over the same course).
> On hearing this, Neill (8:9) runs over to Carol and tries to hit her with a rope.
> *The spectators* shout: Cheat, cheat!
> As Carol crosses the line, *Ginny* (9:0) shouts: She's done it, she's done it, she's won.
> *Neill* tries to deny Carol's success: 'No that was only two times [round]', (redefine the act), but his comments are ignored.

Neill simply had to win and when he once dropped out of a race, because he was out of breath, he did not take kindly to being told, 'You've got to do as many laps as you can'. He tersely replied, 'Too bad'. Neill was trying to give a new interpretation to his actions, by redefining himself from a 'tired person' to an 'independent agent, who can choose at will whether or not to compete'. Even if he was sometimes unsuccessful he had a knack of 'playing with words'; who else would try to get round losing a race by telling his competitor, 'You're just trying to make trouble'?

Intolerance of opposition
Neill's insistence on having control in a game put any common activities into jeopardy. In the following game of 'grandmother's footsteps', Neill tries to remain in the coveted role of grandmother for as long as possible, and does so with more than just skilful play. First, he uses physical violence and threatens exclusion, then he changes one of the rules of the game and no longer stays beside the wall but wanders some feet away. It seems that he is intent on showing how easily he can remain in the role of grandmother. But the more Neill shows off, the more likely the break up of the game becomes. When the other children challenge him and begin to walk away, Neill courts them with a compromise and offers to start the game again.

> *Neill* is the grandmother and stands with his face to the wall. He turns round: Carol (see you).
> *Carol*: Frank pushed (deny agency).
> She stays where she is and does not go back to the wall.
> *Mary* (to Neill): That's not fair, you're not allowed to do that.
> Neill had not returned back to the grandmother's wall before turning to face the other participants. Mike

reaches the grandmother's wall and Neill grabs him and
pushes him back.
Neill: You're not playing, everyone back against the
wall, back to the beginning.
They all go back.
Neill sends Ramesh back, but he doesn't go and the
game continues.
Neill: Bond, back, you bent your knees, see how you moved.
Pete: You're making them move   (deny agency).
John touches the wall.
Neill: I got you, go back to your place. John complies.
To Pete: You go back, Bond.
Pete: I did go back.
Neill: You're not allowed to go till I turn round,
I'm warning you.
 Ramesh, you're not allowed to move.
 You're not allowed to do that   (Pete has just
run up to the wall).
Frank (to Neill): You're just making this up.

As grandmother, Neill walks round all over the place instead
of staying at the wall. Soon everyone rushes to the wall
regardless of whether Neill has his back turned and the game
breaks down. Neill gets the game going again by suggesting
a compromise. He starts them all in a line about three feet
from the wall, at last giving them a chance to win. Very
soon John becomes the new grandmother.

On many other occasions Neill's insistence on having his own
way caused the game to break up. When this happened he was
careful to shift the blame onto someone else, as in the next
episode.

Neill: You've got to run trackways, you can't do that,
you can't turn back.
John: That's your rules.
Neill: He's not playing, he's breaking the rules.
We were going to play until John spoiled the rules.
We can't play, none of you can.
John (to other children): Let's go somewhere else.

Avoiding fights
I have already suggested that being tough brings respect,
particularly among boys at Middle School. Neill was not obviously
the strongest in the playground and thus would be unlikely to
win fights automatically. In fact, he seemed at great pains to
avoid fights and I never saw him fighting either at First or at
Middle School. He was, however, determined to be seen as tough
and even gave himself the nickname 'the Fonz', modelling himself on the 'super-cool' television hero. Interestingly, he
managed to make this name stick and many children

spontaneously told me that 'Neill's the Fonz'.

His dedication not to be seen to give in during verbal battles, while at the same time avoiding fighting, can be seen in the following long episode, which was collected over a twenty minute period during a midday playtime. First, a synopsis of the plot,

Neill and a few other boys have been disrupting the girls' game of 'roll over.' Neill's insistence on joining in as captain was the last straw. The girls throw verbal abuse at the boys, which they faithfully return. The sexes call each other names, glare and claim that they could easily inflict some terrible harm, such as the breaking of fingers or the smashing of skulls. Two rather conflicting accusations are flung between children. 'I'm not scared of you' reveals the value attached to a lack of fear, while 'He wants a fight' shows that the actual initiation of violence is frowned upon. Nobody, it seems, wants an all-out fight, but equally nobody wants to be seen to give in. This leads to a stalemate from which there seems no way out of the accusation/counter-accusation routine.

At this point Neill produces a most striking solution. He pretends to go to sleep, and as the girls around continued to taunt him, his definition catches on with the other boys. In this way the problem is solved. An all out fight is avoided, and the boys are not seen to be giving in, for 'sleeping dogs do not have to answer to bitches' taunts'. But as we shall see the girls do not give up that easily. Eventually an end to playtime terminates the episode; the adult world has intervened. Surprising though it may seem, the social upheaval caused by this battle was quickly glossed over and the following lunchtime I only heard brief references to the 'events' of the previous day.

Pete (9:4) (accidentally) knocks over Jane (8:10).
Jane gets really angry, and glares at him, hits him, and now chases after Neill.
Jane: Neill is a baby, Neill is a baby.
Neill, Pete and some other boys are trying to disrupt the girls' game of 'roll over'.
Jane: Just because he can't be captain (about Neill).
Now the girls all start chasing the boys.
Graeme (9:3) rushes up to Ginny (9:0) and gets down on his knees: Spare me, spare my life! (redefine the situation - real to pretend).
Ginny: Not sure that I will.
Ginny to Neill: Big Ears, spoilsport, he wants a fight.
John has been knocked over in a scuffle and on regaining his feet goes after Ginny.
John: I'll get you.
John 'paces' Ginny round the playground; as he walks he glares and Ginny recedes backwards.

John: I'm not scared of you.
Ginny: I'm not scared of anybody.
John: Flubbadubba, and a smile appears on his face,
(redefine the situation – real to pretend).
Ginny: Look, he soon changes his tune (thwarts attempt
to change definition of situation).
John regains his glare and goes off (he can either fight
or withdraw).
The children are in two groups by sex and each starts
chanting:
Boys: What are little girls made of?
Girls: What are little boys made of?
After a moment,
Neill (to Ginny): Who's scared of you now?
Ginny: Neill's got a little dust on him.
Jane: One of the loonies has escaped.
Jane and Pete tussle.
Pete: I could have broken your fingers.
Jane: I could have broken yours as well.
Now Pete tussles with Ginny, who says, He's scared of me
anyday.
Ginny (to the other girls): They're scared of my little hands.
Ginny to Clare (9:2): I want to do like that , and she slaps
her hand down in the air.
Ginny to Pete: He's scared of me, he's scared of me, he's
a baby.
Pete: Who's scared ?, and Ginny gently punches him on
the cheek.
Pete: I'm not scared.
Meanwhile, in the background a number of the boys and girls
are announcing their impressions (i.e. play acting) of certain
members of the opposite sex.
John to Pete: Here's an impression of Pete Bond.
Pete: Look, you're on my side, you dummy.
Meanwhile Neill tells Ginny: I'm not ticklish .
Ginny: Oh no, put your arm up, itchy bum.
Pete: Get down there, sit down there , and he pushes
Carole (7:8) to the ground.
Jane: You could have broken her skull doing that.
Pete: Yeah?
The two glare at each other. Pete lets his coat drop
from around his shoulders (it looks like in preparation for
action) and Ginny smiles and says: Batman, Batman and
Pete and Jane smile at each other, (redefine situation).
Neill now lies down on the ground and Ginny, Carol and Sara
all say, He likes this, he likes this , as they place their
feet on his prostrate body.
Jane: He don't like this , and she puts her feet over his
groin and Sara does the same.
Ginny: Ah, Garratt's (Neill) surrendered at last, he's
ticklish.

Pete gets down on the ground to join Neill.
Clare: Overgrown baby.
Dinner-lady comes over to Neill and Pete, Get up.
Ginny: It started just because he couldn't be the captain
of 'roll over', he starts making war, he starts bashing us in.
Dinner-lady: Go on, get up, you silly boys.
Neill: Miss, I want to sleep.
Dinner-lady: Come on, children want to run round, they'll
fall over you.
Neill goes over to the corner of the playground and lies
down. The girls follow him over.
Carol: When he sits down, he's got a split in his bum
like this.
Ginny: Oh, we want to see his face , since Neill has
covered his face with a coat.
Carol: Oh, what a silly face.
Neill, Pete and Graeme all pretend it is bedtime and pay no
attention to the girls. They say Goodnight to each other.
Carol sticks her foot on Neill's head and then his tummy.
Joy and Sara kick Neill on the side.
Ginny: Look what you lot have done.
Neill: I never.
Ginny: Touch me, so I hope to die, that shows you ain't
going to touch them any more.
Sara (8:3) puts her foot out.
Neill grabs Carol: Now I've got you, you bastard, you
just shut up bothering us.
Carol: I'm telling Miss.
Ginny: No, I ain't going to leave you alone, not now.
I'm going to annoy him all the time; I will, don't worry.
Carol slams her foot down on Neill.
Four girls sing: Baby, baby on the treetop, when the
bough breaks the baby will fall , etc.
Neill still pretends to be asleep.
Ginny: My talons would scratch you to pieces.
Jane tries to touch his groin.
Clare hits Neill all over with a wooden spoon and he
lies doggo.
Graeme attacks Clare and wrestles the spoon off her and
hits her with it. He misses Clare and hits Sara.
Beckie: Give that to me, it's not yours, it's mine.
Jane wrenches the spoon off Graeme and gives it to Beckie.
Clare: It's probably got poison on it.
Ginny: He opened his eyes (Neill), he ain't dead, what
a shame.
Neill: I'll tell you where you can't disturb us, (to boys)
come on, you lot, let's get off.
Pete, Neill, Graeme and John all go to the boys' toilets.
Clare: I tell you what, I tell you what, upstairs you can
see the boys in the toilets.
Another girl: We're not allowed upstairs.

Clare: I know, I know.
Carol forays into the boys' toilets (or at least the area of them) and announces: Eeh, Neill Garratt's doing a piss-piss, his piss-piss is green.
When the boys emerge from the toilets *Graeme* says to Helen Let's have a staring match, see who can outstare each other.
Neill complains to the dinner-lady: Carol keeps on coming into the boys' toilets.
Dinner-lady tells Carol: Don't go there.
Neill: See, see, don't tell fibs.
Graeme 'paces' Carol around the playground and they glare at each other. Carol backs away. When she runs to the other side of the playground she shouts: Scaredy boots, Welly boots .
Neill goes back to 'sleep' with Pete.
Mary (8:9): Playing Mummies and Daddies, are you?
Neill and John get hold of Mary and pull her down.
John: Look what I've got, look what I've got.
(John has captured Carol)
Carol: I'm telling Miss.
John punches Carol and lets her go.
Neill: Let her go, I'm going to sleep.
Carol: Don't touch us again, Welly boots.
Clare: Look at his fat bum.
Beckie: Oy, Ginny, they're all snug and warm.
Jane, Ginny, Carol, Helen, Beckie and Sara are the girls now involved.
Ginny: Look at the little babies asleep, do you want your bottles?
Mary: Bond, Bond, Miss wants you.
(Pete takes no notice).
Neill: Why don't you go away?
Ginny: No, you started annoying us, now we're going to annoy you.
Neill: Miss, we can't get any peace.
Ginny: You shouldn't have annoyed us in the first place.
The boys smell a pungent odour.
Neill: Who's done it?
In turn the boys go 'taxi, taxi, taxi', which with the appropriate sign of thumb on tongue, and then dabbed on forehead with the palm outstretched, is the ritual means to deny responsibility for the smell.
Graeme touches a dead frog that he sees and as all the other boys shout, 'Welland's got the lurgi' the whistle calls an end to playtime.

At Middle School
Along with ten of his peers, nine-year-old Neill progressed from First to Middle School and I observed him in this new environment to see how his reputation as 'boss' would fare.

There were two observation periods of all ten children from First School in their Middle School playground. The first was for three weeks at the start of their first term and the second for two weeks at the start of their second term at Middle School. It was during this term that I talked to each of them about playtime. In addition, I observed Neill for two weeks at the end of his first year at Middle School.

On arrival at Middle School, Neill was clearly nervous and during the first day he was the only child in his class to spend parts of it quietly sobbing. It seems that the other children realized this for they told the teachers at his old school. He was also worried about what to do at playtime and asked the class teacher, 'Can we play football at playtime?' 'Yes, in the big playground' was her reply, and he complained, 'But the big boys are playing there'. He was generally unsure of himself during this first week in the playground and in the next episode complained to a teacher that 'there's nothing to do.'

Neill and a few boys are trying to disrupt a girls' racing game of 'Oxford and Cambridge' by sitting down as if they were participants.
Girls: Get out, get out. Miss, Miss, tell these boys to stop joining in (without permission). The boys go off and *Neill* says to the teacher,
Miss, Miss, there's nothing to do.
His comment is ignored.

Unlike Neill's acknowledged status at First School, none of his peers that I talked to at Middle School referred to him as the 'boss', either at the beginning or at the end of the first year. Most of them, including Neill, mentioned the big boys (the twelve- and thirteen-year-olds) as the 'bosses', 'they're the ones who control the playground.' Neill told me he preferred the First School's playground where, 'We was bigger and could do what we want. Nobody could get in our way or anything. Here, they're bigger and they're bossy.'

Any power that Neill did have was much less than at First School. For example, to join in a game, I now saw him always ask, 'Can I play?', and he was sometimes excluded. On one such occasion he tried bribery, but was unsuccessful.

Neill (9:2): Let's play, Javed?
Javed (9:0): 'No.
Neill: I'll give you a sweet.'
Javed: Let's see, and he looks at it for some moments before replying No. Neill walks off.

Even during his first few weeks at Middle School, Neill showed the same style of interaction as at First School. He was keen to show how good he was at racing and football, intolerant of any opposition during games and still avoided fighting.

Races and football
Although there was no evidence from my playground observation that neither Neill nor any of the other children at Middle School considered racing to be important for building a reputation, the class teacher told me about what happened on Sports Day.

> Neill lost a race and was very unhappy about it. He sulked and then went through the whole thing of saying that someone tripped him up or got in his way. In another race when he realized that he wasn't going to come in the first three he dropped out, he said he'd got a bad leg and limped off. But it obviously wasn't bad because he was fine after that. He wants to win. If he doesn't win, then it doesn't help with his (feeling of) popularity, because he feels that getting in the first three adds to his prowess. If he doesn't win, then he sulks and is disappointed in himself.

As far as football was concerned, Neill's comments on his first day at Middle School revealed that he obviously wanted to play football, but perceived it as the prerogative of the older boys. During the first few weeks none of the new children played football, but when I returned the following term a curious change had occurred. Every playtime a line of about thirty boys of all ages would spread out along a wall and wait to be picked to play. First, the owner of the ball would choose two captains and then they in turn would decide which of them should have the first pick, using the 'hammer and nails' method that I described in Chapter 3. Usually about half of the boys were successful in their bid to join in and nearly all of these were eleven- or twelve-year-olds. Neill, however, unlike most boys of his age was picked quite often. He told me that he had not immediately started playing with the 'big kids' because 'they didn't know if I was good enough; but one day they picked me and (found out that) I was quite good.'
Does an ability to play football well enhance one's reputation? The fact that practically every playtime large numbers of young boys attempted to be picked to play with the older ones supports this idea. If prestige were not involved, and all that these children wanted was a game of football, then they would hardly stand about in a line, but instead proceed directly to their usual destination, that of a football game between children of their own age in one of the crowded corners of the playground.

Intolerance of opposition
Just as in First School, Neill was prepared to withdraw from a game in order to make the point that he was not prepared to play with 'troublemakers'. In the following argument, Neill withdrew from the game even after he had won his case not to be 'it'.

In tig-off-ground:
Neill tigs *Garth*, who denies being touched,
No.
Garth and *Ben*, about Neill: He's it.
Neill: No, I'm not.
Ben: Weren't we all off-ground?
Garth: Neill Garratt, I'm not it. Garrtie Eyes,
you're it.
Neill (to John): I'm just going to pack the game up,
if they're not playing (properly).
John (to other boys): It doesn't take much to be it.
Garth: Hey you, Garrtie Eyes, Neill Garrtie Eyes
is it.
Neill: I ain't.
Garth: Go on then, tig me then.
Garth takes the role of 'it'. He has lost
his argument with Neill and tries to pull John
from an off-ground position.
John: I'll beat you up.
Neill to John: Look, we'll have a bit of fun.
Both go off.

Avoiding fights
Being seen to be tough was particularly valued at Middle School
and should a fight break out, it was difficult for the participants
to withdraw from the mêlée, especially when a crowd formed.
Neill told me that their shouts of 'fight, fight' make the fight
go harder, and that just as at First School he went to some
lengths to avoid physical conflict. He explained to me in private,
'I don't like fighting, because I always come out badly bruised.'
   In the episode below, from the beginning of the second term,
Neill and Nick are in conflict over who is in goal. Neill ignores
Nick's overtures to fight, and instead attempts to swing the
other players round to his interpretation - that Nick has
usurped his rightful place in goal.

Tim: I'm going in goal.
Neill (in goal): You get lost, you.
John: I'll go in goal.
Neill: No you don't (and he stays in goal).
Nick: I'm in goal.
Neill: Oh, shut up.
Nick tries to grab the ball from Neill's hands.
Neill: Get out!
Nick: Fuck off!
Neill: No.
Bob goes up to Nick.
Nick: Piss off! and pushes Bob away.
Bob hits Nick, but then smiles and pushes him gently,
(redefine situation).
Nick glares, pushes Bob, Bob goes off.

Nick approaches Neill, Neill retreats a couple of feet
and Nick takes up a position in goal. At this stage
it's still not clear who's in goal.
Nick announces: I'm in goal .
Neill: No, he ain't, if he handballs it....
(Neill decides not to fight but tries to get the others
to accept his definition). When Nick picks up the ball,
Neill shouts: Handball!-
Another boy takes a free kick.
Neill says to an older boy: You tell him (i.e. Nick).
Nick: No, I'm in goal.
Chris (12): Get out of the way, you Paki (to Nick),
and kicks the ball at him. This shot misses, and Chris
grabs Nick, and pushes him out of the way.
Nick grins and *Chris* says: Watch it, Nicky.
Nick is smiling and grinning and says, No .
Nick is now in goal and saves the free kick.
Neill shouts: Oh, come on, Nick!
Another boy tries to drag Nick away and there is a
small tussle.
The penalty is retaken.
Neill: Come on, get out of goal now, Nick.
Nick: No.
Neill has now left the goal.
Nick: I'm in this (goal).
Neill concedes defeat: All right then.
Meanwhile a *little boy* shouts from the background:
 Get stuck in the aggro.

Although Neill failed to get his own way, he made a valiant
attempt to keep Nick out of goal using words alone.
   In the next episode from the start of the second term, Neill
resists even more strongly the invitation to fight. When presented with the boy, who had a few minutes before made him
cry, he steadfastly ignores his friends pleas to 'punch him
back'. So instead they punish the offender on Neill's behalf.

Neill is seen crying by himself at the side of the
playground.
Nick grabs Wally and brings him to Neill.
Wally: I've said sorry.
Graeme: Come on, Garratt, punch him back in the tummy now.
Wally: I said sorry.
Neill disregards these requests and looks straight ahead
trying to ignore everything.
Nick: Come on, Garratt, punch him back.
Graeme is trying to drag Neill towards Wally: Go on,
punch him, hit him.
Wally runs off.
Neill is left by himself sobbing, and Nick and Graeme
capture Wally again, and drag him back to Neill.

They tell Neill: Come on, Neill, punch him, punch him.
Wally: Get lost.
Neill walks off and ignores this.
Graeme and Nick start beating up Wally by themselves
with *Wally* shouting, Get lost.
A dinner-lady arrives on the scene and says: I don't
think he likes it.
Wally (to dinner-lady): He's accused me of something.
Dinner-lady (to all the children): Don't be so silly,
stop it.
The fight breaks up.

About twenty minutes later I talked to Neill and asked him,
'What was the problem?' He was surprisingly off-hand about the
whole affair. 'Oh, nothing much, it was during a game, he
(Wally) came up to me with his fists up and I thought he wanted
to fight, so I shouted, "Shut up, you Wally Gaitor", so he
punched me in the Adam's apple.'

After one year at Middle School
When I watched Neill at the end of his third term at Middle
School, I noticed some changes. Unlike his time at First School,
and to some extent his early days at Middle School, he was now
more prepared to accept opposition, concerning, for example,
role selection or what games to play. It seemed that he was
beginning to come to terms with not being able to get his own
way so easily, and not being recognized as the 'boss' meant
that his presence was no longer so sought after. No matter how
many times he threatened to withdraw from a game, on each
occasion it was ignored.

In a game of 'peep-behind-the-curtain' ('grandmother's
footsteps'), Neill thinks that he's qualified to be the
grandmother, but is told:
 You've got to go back (to the wall) and come back up
(start again).
Neill: Oh, I'm not playing this game.
No reaction from the other players and he quickly
joins in again.
A minute later:
Neill: I'm not going back to the wall, he just says it
(that he's seen me moving) because he wants to keep being
'it' (the 'grandmother') all the time. I'm not playing.
Again he rejoins the game, after no reaction.
After a few more minutes:
Neill kicks a girl to make her move.
Nick: You cheated, Neill.
Neill: No, I never moved.
Nick: Oh, get back, I got all you lot.
Neill: I ain't playing.
This time the game breaks down, but not because of Neill,

but because the children are tired of Nick retaining the
'grandmother' role for so long, and they all walk off.

An even more noticeable change was the extent to which Neill
refrained from becoming involved in even the most obvious
arguments that went on around him. Being so subdued was in
sharp contrast to previously, when he could almost be guaranteed to be in with the 'action', wherever it was. Yet old habits
die hard. I still often saw Neill harshly criticize others, order
them about and pass judgment:

> *Neill* to a goalkeeper who has just let in a goal:
> He's scared of the ball.

But, unlike before, he now received as much as he gave:

> *Jack* to Neill: You're in goal.
> *Neill*: I'm not, I'm not, he's in, (pointing to another
> boy).
> *Jack*: At least he's not a little baby, like you.
> *Neill*: I'm not a baby, I (just) don't like going in goal.
> Neill walks off.

> *Di*: The tallest stand up.
> Neill stands up together with Fina, who is easily taller.
> *Neill*: I'm taller, I'm taller than you, sit down,
> (and he pushes Fina down).
> *Di*: Shut up, Neill, you're not the taller.
> You can call next time, if you sit down and play
> properly.
> Neill complies.

Gaining a reputation as 'boss' of the playground
How did Neill manage to gain a reputation as 'boss' of the First
School playground and why did he not have the same reputation
at Middle School? One important feature of his character was
quite simply the extent to which he was determined to be the
'boss'. It seems that in First School he announced he was the
'boss', and the others accepted it. His class teacher put it like
this:

'Neill wanted to be accepted as a leader but he didn't
really have the character to be like that. He tried to
buy it, to some extent, with sweets. They said, in effect,
"Well, he wants to be leader, so we'll let him and accept
him as such." He wasn't a natural leader, the others found
him amusing, which wasn't quite the respect that he wanted.
He pushed for leadership by organizing them, but the others
didn't take too much notice of him unless they wanted to.'

Neill's class teacher at Middle School also noticed that he was much more interested in what his peers thought of him than in her opinion. This proved an obstacle to effective learning:

'He's very chatty; you think he's brighter than he is, he can give a lot of information verbally, but he can't get a lot down. He doesn't listen to instructions. He can't concentrate; he always seems to have so much to say and he's always going to do such a lot, but when he actually does it he might have done it wrong, because he hasn't heard what you meant in the first place, or because he's been nattering to other people. Yet he's got a fantastic imagination for stories, but he never actually gets it down. He could be quite good, but he never produces anything.'

Neill's style of interacting bears most similarity to the descriptions by Montagner and Manning of outgoing teasers. Although he was full of exciting new ideas about what to play, he was also determined to be in control and was intolerant of any opposition. His hostility was clearly aimed at showing, both to himself and to others, that he could be boss. Unlike many of the teasers at Nursery School, his hostility was far more verbal than physical. Even when he was friendly to his playmates, and offered them sweets, he did so in such a way as to emphasize his control over them.

On one occasion at Middle School he announced: 'Ooh, look, I've got something in my pocket. Nobody look!', and he put this mysterious object into one of his clenched fists. He then placed his fists out in front and asked his two playmates to choose a fist each. The one who chose correctly was allowed to keep the sweets.
On another occasion Neill was seen walking around in conversation with two boys when he suddenly withdrew a half-empty sweet packet from his pocket and threw it on the ground, commanding 'Scramble, scramble'! His two friends grovelled in an effort to beat each other to the food.

One of the characteristics of teasers that Manning has noted is that they are not very original in the way they solve problems. They tend to use the same solution time and time again, even if it was clearly not effective the first time. To be fair, Neill was a bit more original than that - who else would dare fall asleep during an argument with the girls? But he too at times repeatedly tried the same unsuccessful strategy, for example, threatening to withdraw from a game. When he was acknowledged as the 'boss' at First School, this tactic worked, but it was less successful at Middle School.
What happened to Neill's status and power as 'boss' when he went up to Middle School? His reputation, it appears, did not go with him and during his first year there Neill made no obvious

attempts to claim he was the 'boss'. This was partly a recognition of the fact that he was now a small fish in a big pond, and
he confided that he preferred the First School playground
precisely because, 'We was bigger and we could do what we
want.' In addition, he now had to compete in Middle School with
many more boys of his own age, and even he begrudgingly
told me that 'there's not a "boss" (in our class), but there is
a best person, who's best at everything.' In case I should get
the wrong impression he quickly added: 'He's a bighead, but
he's small (really).' Nearly all his classmates, however, recognized Adrian as the 'boss', though I saw no such acknowledg-
ment in the playground. According to the class teacher, Adrian
was clearly brighter than the others and although Neill was
popular, 'He did not have the same initiative to get people
organized.'

Neill's story is far from complete. Although at the end of his
first year at Middle School he was much more subdued in the
playground, his behaviour in class suggests that he had not
lost the motivation to be in control. It will be interesting to
see what happens in the future. It may be that when he's
thirteen-years-old, and at the top of the school, he will make
another attempt to be the 'boss'. David Hargreaves records
how one fifteen-year-old, Clint, rose to be 'cock' of the
comprehensive school where he taught in Lancashire. Clint's
methods were not unlike Neill's. He spread his claim to be
'cock' on the basis of several small incidents, such as beating
up a prefect, and sought to make himself easily observable as
'hard' or 'tough' by a process of self-display. As another boy
put it: 'People are afraid of you if you go swaggering round
the playground.' Lastly, he managed to avoid fights, because
there was no single boy who was willing to challenge him. My
guess is that Neill will attempt a come-back. Personality styles
show remarkable endurance, particularly when there are no
major changes in the child's environment.

8

That's how we learn'

> During playtime Jon (5) is talking to one of the
> workmen repairing a path just outside the playground:
> *Jon:* We're watching you, we're watching you.
> *Workman:* But are you learning.
> *Jon* (after a few moments' thought): That's how
> we learn.

Only nine months earlier the same little boy had told me that
playtime makes you grow up extremely slowly. He is much older
now, and even more eloquent, and it is his perceptive comments
that I want to examine in this chapter. What is there to learn
in the playground and how important are the lessons?

In the last five chapters I have shown that there is order
amongst the apparent chaos of the playground. In describing
the activities, problems, and solutions of five- to ten-year-old
children I have indicated some of the skills that they display at
playtime. They recognize themselves as one amongst others,
perceive other people's intentions and manage to organize their
own behaviour appropriately. The fact that they are able to do
so suggests an understanding, implicit or explicit, of the
structure of the society of which they are all members. They
realize that different people occupy different roles and that
there are standards and values, which govern relationships
between these roles.

To what extent does developing this awareness of how to
interact at playtime prepare a child for coping in the adult
world? There are two issues here. First, are the means by which
the social world of the playground is created and maintained
essentially similar to those by which adults create and sustain
their worlds? Second, is experience in the playground a necessary stage to ensure 'normal' development? I shall show that
there are many similarities, and that although it is impossible
ever to be certain, all the evidence points to the vital
importance of peer experience, and the playground provides
a major opportunity for it.

WHAT DO CHILDREN LEARN IN THE PLAYGROUND?

I have approached the question of what is learned in the playground by observing the skills that children display there,
both in their games and in the social problems that continually

arise. This does not, of course, tell us anything about how and when these skills develop. Do they come about due to the influence of peer interaction within the playground, or are they already present, even before the child starts school? Who learns what, when and how must depend, in part at least, on individual characteristics, such as age, sex, developmental stage and personality style.

Life in the playground involves the learning of numerous specific skills that are required in order to master and excel at a particular game or solve a particular social problem. But the children may be learning much more than is immediately obvious. Some of the skills, attitudes and beliefs acquired at playtime might transfer or generalize to other non-playground situations. Although my first ideas about the importance of playtime concerned whether there might be any playground skills, which transfer to the classroom (e.g. whether hopscotch helps the learning of number skills, whether choosing 'it' introduces children to the concept of a random number), I quickly became much more interested in the lessons of playtime that might be relevant for adult life.

In order to identify which playtime skills might transfer to adulthood, we need to have a fairly detailed knowledge of what adults do. As adults ourselves we, of course, know a good deal about the management of social interaction in its many different settings - in families, offices, pubs, tea parties, to name but a few. There are many worlds of adulthood and there are two levels at which we can make comparisons between them and life in the playground. In terms of specific learning, can we see the same strategies being used to solve problems? In terms of more general learning, are the attitudes, beliefs and values fostered at playtime a good preparation for adult life?

STRATEGIES DURING DISPUTES: PLAYING WITH WORDS

Games play an important role in children's development, because they offer the creation of an order which can easily break down, bringing with it the opportunity to initiate, discuss, influence and change the rules. The ways children manipulate each other, both in games and more generally at playtime, are much the same as the strategies used by adults and many of these subtle techniques can even be seen at Nursery School.

Much of my research has been about the ways children manipulate each other with words, though often the same goal might be achieved by an equivalent non-verbal strategy. The techniques rest upon the fact that although we might know what we intend, others may interpret our actions differently. Sometimes we feel the need to clarify the meaning of our actions. At other times we might offer a new interpretation of either what we or someone else has done, aiming perhaps to excuse our own action or lack of it. These techniques of the playground should be familiar to us as adults, but more surprising perhaps is that they can be traced right back to the Nursery School, where three- to five-year-olds are likewise in a world set up and controlled by adults, but where they are left more or less alone to do what they want with companions of roughly the same age.

Four-year-olds frequently restate the definition of the situation, telling each other, for example: 'It's only pretend.' They also argue about the implications that each believes stem from the definition. For instance, in a fantasy about boats I saw one child insist: 'If that's the sea you musn't walk on it.' But in order to get his own way, the playmate claimed magical powers and walked across the water. In just the same way, at playtime, six-year-old Shweta successfully redefined herself as too young to be able to follow the rules of hopscotch. Adults also try to hide behind the way they present themselves to others, frequently claiming to be in some respect incompetent so as to avoid a task or having to make a decision.

Redefining the context within which an action is interpreted is also a tactic at the Nursery School. I recently, saw a four-year-old boy rush into a fight and tell the antagonist: 'I'm the doctor, stop it Colin.' Unfortunately, his attempt to place the fight within a fantasy episode, in which he had a controlling role, was ignored, just like the suggestion of an eight-year-old girl to Nick that he 'Cry mercy' during a fight. The whole group then proceeded to treat the fight as if it were a wrestling match. Similarly, adults might try to pretend that a fight was merely a friendly tussle, so as to avoid feeling obliged to intervene.

Lastly, individuals of all ages are capable of denying that they were responsible for an action, or indeed that it happened at all. These are both examples of what Sigmund Freud called defence mechanisms - projecting our own deeds onto others and totally repressing any memory for the event. One little boy at Nursery School, for example, pushed his playmate's car away and when challenged claimed: 'It went by itself, I saw it go by itself.'

Children, like adults, are constantly trying to get their own way, whilst being careful not to manipulate to such an extent as to be excluded from the group. This was the fate of nine-year-old Nick who, once he had gained a reputation for being violent, was frequently denied entry into games of football. When he hit out in retaliation, this served to strengthen the group's resolve and they told him: 'Now you're certainly not playing.' A more effective strategy might have been to attempt to bribe them with: 'Do you wanna sweet?', or to suggest an exciting new game that would attract others to him.

Some children know just how far to go and when to stop. When two eight-year-old boys barged into a girls' game of 'grandmother's footsteps', they proceeded to play very roughly, took giant steps when the 'grandmother's' back was turned, and

pushed others over so that their victims would be told to go
back to the wall and start again. Just as the boys were nearing
the 'grandmother', a little girl arrived and asked, 'Can I play?'
The 'grandmother' agreed and announced: 'Everyone back to the
wall'. To my surprise, although the two boys voiced their dis-
appointment, they meekly complied with her request. They
seemed to know that if they wanted the game to continue then
they could not go against the rules at will, or the game would
break down.

INSULTS, THREATS AND BRIBES

Many of the ways in which children and adults manipulate each
other are similar, but there are also differences in the tactics
of each age group. One difference is that although some children at Nursery School, notably the teasers, continually give
out conflicting messages about whether their intentions are
friendly or aggressive, they do not seem to be deliberately
trying to cause confusion. It is not that young children cannot
switch quickly from one situation or mood to another, but rather
that they have not yet mastered how to manipulate others by
doing so.
  Nicknaming, like the ability to give deliberately conflicting
information, is also a strategy of the First and Middle School.
There are names based on physical peculiarities (fatso, four
eyes), puns or parodies of the child's own name (Welly boots
for Welland), names based on social relationships (a younger
brother becomes minor) and names based on mental traits (dumbo,
brains). In his book 'Word Play', Peter Farb suggests that 'the
insults spoken by adults are usually more subtle than the simple
name-calling used by children, but children's insults make
obvious some of the verbal strategies people carry into adult
life. Most parents engage in wishful thinking when they regard
name-calling as good-natured fun which their children will soon
grow out of. Name-calling is not good-natured and children do
not grow out of it; as adults they merely become more expert
in its use.'
  The same is true for the way adults threaten and bribe each
other. In Nursery and First School threats abound: 'I won't
be your friend', 'I'll give you a sweet if you let me play'. Adults,
on the other hand, tend to keep such tactics for dire emergen-
cies, and when they do bribe or threaten they are usually much
more subtle. They impart their message in such a roundabout
way that if challenged, they can easily claim to have been
misunderstood. Even if children have not learnt such a degree
of subtlety in their spoken threats, many seven-year-olds have
mastered this sophistication in the way they use a particular
facial gesture, that Gail Zivin has called the 'plus' face.
  From her observations in the United States, Zivin has noticed
a facial expression made by some four- to ten-year-olds as they

enter a dispute. The child who makes it is very likely to get
his or her own way, and because the expression predicts the
winner so well, Zivin called it the 'plus' face. It involves raising
the eyebrows and chin and holding the eyes wide open in
apparent direct eye contact with the victim. She noticed it most
often in the repertoire of the dominant children, particularly
among the seven- to ten-year-olds. It is probable that the child
who makes a 'plus' face is not doing so consciously, but rather
as part of a more general self-confident air and posture.

Even more interesting is the difference between the four and
ten years in when and how the face is made. Dominant seven-
to ten-year-olds almost never gave the 'plus' face during
obviously aggressive encounters, but gave it instead during
even-tempered conversations. The face had changed its context.
Among the four- and five-year-olds it had been seen in disputes
involving objects and locations, winning freedom from someone
demanding you do something, and gaining recognition as the
winner after an argument. Now it was being used to emphasize
points that were being made, and when doing something that
was considered difficult, because of a dare or request from
another child. Even though the top-ranking younger children
also showed the 'plus' face in these non-aggressive situations,
the way they made the face was different; they held it longer
and so it was much more clearly noticeable.

Zivin was impressed by the sophistication of some of the older
children and suggests that they have mastered one of the social
skills of adulthood. The more dominant older children were
using a facial gesture to create an aura of challenge, and
because the 'plus' face was too swift to be noticed as an isolated
act (unless one has seen it stand out in the behaviour of
younger children), it was difficult for the victim to complain.
By threatening at a level below conscious awareness, the children were able to manipulate without risking exclusion from the
group.

TEASING BETWEEN THE SEXES

Boys and girls at First and Middle School frequently tease each
other. They push, pull, poke and imitate in a way that Nursery
School children would not tolerate. Such intrusion would make
the younger ones feel threatened and they would either cry,
withdraw, fight back or appeal to the teacher for help. Older
children obviously enjoy the teasing, for they choose to interpret ambiguous physical contact as friendly, and often turn it
into a game. This is despite the fact that in public boys and
girls will pour scorn on each other. The attraction of teasing,
and games like 'kiss chase', is that they allow children to give vent
to a growing interest in the opposite sex. But in both activities,
they still have to be wary not to be seen to enjoy themselves.
A boy will only let himself be kissed by the girl who catches him

after a symbolic struggle. But, as children pass through
puberty, the attitudes that can be seen in teasing and 'kiss
chase' become more and more a part of everyday life.

RITUAL

Just as an interest in teasing and 'kiss chase' comes about
because of the children's developmental stage, so too do the
rituals of playground life. They are invoked, and often invented,
to answer children's needs in the playground. Although their
precise form may vary from place to place, the job they they do
remains the same. This is well illustrated by 'taxi', 'mercy' and
'crucems'. When we examine how the problems that 'bagsee'
solves are coped with, both before and after the playground
world, we shall see how the rituals of playtime prepare children,
not so much to use exactly the same rituals in adulthood, but
more to cope with ritual in general.

'Taxi'
The consuming interest that five- to ten-year-olds have in the
scatological aspects of their bodily functions is not shared either
by preschool children or by adults. It is a passing phase.
Indeed, I recall that when I was at Primary School we talked
about 'SBDs', (farts that were 'silent but deadly'), but I
never had to announce that I was the guilty one and so protect
myself from being hit six times. What I do now depends on the
company I keep. There is certainly no danger that anyone will
attack me if I fail to claim ownership of the nasty smell. As for
denying it, sometimes I attempt to ignore the event, while at
other times I might acknowledge it and offer the apology 'excuse
me'. In exceptionally intimate company, my apology has often
been met with, 'That's all right you're part of the family here'.
   The children could not enlighten me as to the origin of the
'palm-to-nose' gesture that accompanies 'taxi'. Perhaps it is a
variation of the 'cock-a-snook' gesture, where the outstretched
fingers and palm are wiggled from the end of the nose. Adults
and children alike throughout Europe have used this as a sign
of mockery for centuries, though its derivation is also a mystery.
   When I visited a school in Battersea, I noticed that the
community there had its own equivalent to 'taxi' - 'jets', which
was accompanied by two fingers touching each others' thighs.
Children at Primary School obviously enjoy drawing attention to
their own and others' farts and so they invent rituals that do
just this. It does not seem to matter what precise form the ritual
takes.

'Mercy'
The only time we are likely to hear adults seeking 'mercy' is in
films that re-enact medieval contests and even then their
historical accuracy cannot be guaranteed. Hollywood would have

us believe that in feudal times conflicts were always settled by
a contest of strength, rather than by a judiciary. The defeated
contestant was able to avoid death by seeking 'mercy'. Nowadays
the ritual in the judicial system is to ask the Home Secretary
for 'clemency'; the principle is similar, but there is no longer
any moral obligation to offer leniency.

Perhaps it is the influence of television that has introduced
the ritual of 'mercy' into playground contests of strength. I
was a bit surprised that it was limited to the girls at my schools;
they clutched each others' fingers until one cried 'mercy' and
thus conceded defeat. In 'Cider with Rosie', Laurie Lee
describes a ritual that performed more or less the same function
as 'mercy', but was totally different both in form and origin:
'Many a punch-drunk boy in a playground battle, outnumbered
and beaten to his knees, would be heard to cry: "I will not have
it! I'll not, I say! I repeat I will not have it!"' The origin of
this appeal that brought immediate mercy was their terror of a
teacher that they had nicknamed Crabby because,

> She had a sour yellow look, lank hair coiled in earphones, and
> the skin and voice of a turkey. We were all afraid of Miss B; sh
> spied, she pried, she crouched, she crept, she pounced - she
> was a terror .... Each morning was war without declaration no
> one knew who would catch it next .... Shuffling your feet.
> Playing with the desk! A-smirking at that miserable Betty! I
> will not have it. I'll not, I say. I repeat - I will not have it ...
> So we did not much approve of Crabby - though she was
> responsible for our excellent reflexes.

'Crucems'

'Crucems' only appears at around seven years. Before then
children withdraw from a game by saying, 'I'm not playing'.
Since adults do not often play children's games, they have little
need to claim the safety afforded by 'crucems', or any of its
equivalent words. The Opies discuss the long history and
derivation of some of the truce terms that currently divide the
British Isles into nine main territories. They do not, however,
have anything to say about the origin of 'crucems', other than
it is bordered to the South by 'cribs' and 'creases', to the West
by 'cruce', to the North by 'nicks' and to the East by 'fainites'.

Although 'crucems' does not figure in adult speech, the crossing of the fingers which accompanies it does endure as a
protective signal right through to adulthood. According to
Desmond Morris and his colleagues, who have made a study of
the geographical distribution of gestures, this signal is common
throughout North-West Europe, with Britain as its stronghold.
They were told of three types of protective messages carried
by crossed fingers: good luck, defence against bad luck, and
cancelling a lie. Protection is thus afforded against the failure
of something good happening in the future, against the likeli-
hood of something bad happening in the future, and against
the consequences of something bad that is being done now.

The gesture is said to be derived from the sign of the cross. In South-Eastern Europe, crossing the fingers carries a completely different meaning. It denotes a couple, or close friendship, and it is my guess that if children in these areas have a ritual formula to obtain temporary safety during a game, then it would not involve crossing the fingers. But, childhood protective signals are not always the same as in adulthood. Scottish and French children do not cross their fingers for safety, instead they put their thumbs up and shout 'barley', 'keys' and in French 'pouce' (flea). 'Thumbs up' is also an adult gesture in these areas, but it has a rather different meaning - that something is 'OK'.

'Bagsee'

I heard 'bagsee' being used in the First School playground for three purposes: to gain precedence of possession of an object or location, to avoid or obtain a role, and to state extra rules in a game. On occasion, adults also invoke 'bagsee', but with them it is said half in jest, for it no longer carries anything like the power that it once had.

There are a number of reasons why ten-year-olds at Middle School use 'bagsee' less than their younger brothers and sisters at First School. It is partly because the children become so skilful in using the ritual that it no longer easily solves their problem. For instance, they might all cry 'bagsee me not it' at the same time, or one clever individual might claim the ultimate in ritual of 'bagsee no bagsees'. In addition, the demise of traditional games in this age group means that there are now fewer occasions when 'bagsee' might be appropriate. But, the children are also changing in their attitude towards their peers. Some are becoming more aware of status and simply would not dare challenge the 'toughest' boys in this way, while others are developing an adult-like concern to avoid being seen as greedy or selfish. This too is the age when attitudes towards rules in general are changing. Piaget, in his study of marbles, noted that ten- and eleven-year-olds are beginning to appreciate that rules are merely arbitrary conventions that can be altered, provided that all the players agree to abide by them.

PRESCHOOL CHILDREN

What about children under five, how do they solve the problems in which their elders invoke 'bagsee'? Let us look at conflicts over objects and locations. Observations made way back in 1934 by Helen Dawe in a number of United States Nurseries found that property disputes were the most common reason for quarrels among three- to five-year-olds, particularly amongst the youngest of this age group. They usually proceed with pushing, striking and pulling, often in silence or accompanied by crying, forbidding ('you can't have it') and commanding ('give it me').

But the majority of squabbles were settled by the children themselves rather than through teachers' intervention, with one child usually yielding to another's superior force.

There are some children, however, who are not keen to get into a fight and seek a more peaceful solution. Montagner has noticed that when leaders in the crèche and Nursery want an object or a location, or indeed attention or participation in a game, they usually approach another child with their own head bent sideways down towards the shoulders and with a smile on their faces. This sequence of solicitation first starts when the child begins to walk and continues right up into Primary School. This is despite the fact that language occupies a more and more important place in the communication of these older children. Although adults do not use this sequence in their interactions with each other, Montagner did observe it in their communication with young children. I am not sure the extent to which British children also use this gesture. I have only observed it between parents and their babies and never seen it either in First School or in the Nursery. Perhaps this is a cultural difference between Britain and France.

Another way in which some four-year-olds avoid fights, while at the same time getting what they want, is to make up a rule that favours them rather than their playmates. For example, Margaret Manning saw a girl in a dispute over a swing suggest to her competitor, 'Let's each have it for ten goes' and then proceed to count to ten. The other child abided by this rule for two or three rounds, but then began to tease her. In another incident at an Edinburgh Nursery School that John Drout observed, a boy complained to the teacher that he was being prevented from playing on the horse. She appeased him with, 'You can have it in a little while, after you've counted to twenty.' The boy returned to the group around the horse and loudly proclaimed, 'I'll count to twenty, after that it's my turn.' This solution was readily accepted and all the children joined in the count. When twenty was reached, he took his place on the horse and decided that he now had the power to decide who should have the next go. The solution to his problem had been to turn a teacher's suggestion into a rule, and one which worked to his benefit, and would be readily followed by the other children.

It seems, then, that children as young as four are able to accept rules like those in the previous examples, even though they rarely take the initiative in stating them and have not as yet met the more formal rules which I have called rituals. This is exactly what Piaget observed when he talked to three- and four-year-olds playing marbles. They readily accept rules because they see them as sacred and unchangeable, even though they might in practice unintentionally flout them at every turn.

If young children have the capacity to cope with rituals, why did I only hear 'bagsee' and 'crucems' among children seven years and older? The answer probably lies in the extent to which Western culture in general stresses ritual solutions to problems, and the English are by no means the most formal people in the world. Japan is an obvious example of a society, which is far more bound by conventions, and where emotions are much more strictly repressed in favour of rituals. As might be expected, we do indeed see rituals emerging there at a much earlier age than in the West.

'Janken Play'
Kiyoto Umaoka, a psychologist at Waseda University in Tokyo, has observed that in Japan it is commonplace for pairs of three- to five-year-olds to determine priorities, or settle disputes, by waving a closed hand in the air three times, while chanting the meaningless words 'Jan Ken Pon' and then making one of three finger formations. They announce either the two extended fingers of 'hasami' (scissors), or the flat hand of 'kami' (paper), or the clenched fist of 'ishi' (stone); in dialect the words are 'choki', 'pä', 'gu'. If one child produces a different sign from the other, then someone will inevitably win, since it is held that 'stone' blunts and thus beats 'scissors', 'scissors' cut and thus conquer 'paper', and 'paper' wraps round and thus triumphs over 'stone'.

'Paper, scissors, stone' has ancient roots in China. It embodies a view of the interdependency of forces which has been recognized for over two thousand years. It was Tsou Yen (260 BC), a man of immense erudition and imagination, consulted and honoured by rulers and one of the first serious geographers of China, who proposed that the forces could be arranged in order of mutual conquest. He held that (1) wood, in the form of a plough, overcomes (2) earth, which by damming and constraint, conquers (3) water, which by quenching, overcomes (4) fire, which by melting liquefies (5) metal, which in turn, cuts (1) wood. This Taoist view of the balance of nature has to some extent been replaced by the concepts of yin and yang, but both views remain central to the continuing practice of the five element theory of traditional Chinese acupuncture and seems also to have survived to this day in the guise of Janken play.

The game was introduced into Japan during the Edo period (about 1690), but just when it came to Britain is not clear. When it did arrive, however, it became a game of the First and Middle School and not of the Nursery. In Japan, children as young as three first start playing it as a game for its own sake, and are taught by their older partners. Many of them can neither judge the outcome of a 'Janken' match nor know how to use it, but they are able to take part, because the older ones are prepared to teach them. By five, it is used both in friendly game situations to assign roles, as well as during angry verbal exchanges, either to determine priority or simply who is the winner of the conflict. It is used in exactly the same way by Japanese adults. Iona and Peter Opie report that it is so ordinary that, 'even professors resort to it to decide, for instance, which of them shall drink the next draught, or which of them wash up afterwards.' Perhaps it is precisely because it is such an ordinary, though important, feature of adult social life in Japan that children do take it up so early.

CHILD AND ADULT RITUALS

'Taxi', 'mercy', 'crucems' and 'bagsee' are all devices to deal with problems that for the children are compelling and important. The rituals enable conflicts to be resolved without anyone having to resort to violence. Adults do not generally find themselves in situations where such a quick solution is required. They do not play games and rarely fight and are normally more prepared to discuss the pros and cons of any dispute. Often they feel able to be rational because they are not emotionally so bound up in wanting to win. This is why the playground rituals generally fail to persist to adulthood. But when adults do get into similar situations as children, then we do indeed see rituals.

Anthropologist Robin Fox lived among the Gaelic-speaking community of Tory Island, off the west coast of Ireland. He observed the way men fight over there and what he describes is essentially a system of rules which have the effect of turning conflicts between grown men into large-scale social events. The fights become rituals, and they are strikingly similar, both to the battles that I watched in the playground, and to the ones that Peter Marsh observed on the football terraces at Oxford United. In all three contexts the justification for fighting often stems from the need to defend one's reputation as 'tough'. On Tory Island, 'He's doing it to show he's a man'; on the football terraces calling someone a 'cunt' forces them to respond so as not to lose face; while in the Middle School, boys are not prepared to suffer being called a 'chicken'.

The principles behind the fights are also alike. The participants have the same two implicit aims; they want to both avoid physical contact, and hence the risk of anyone getting hurt, and they also want to avoid being seen to do so, and thus maintain a reputation of toughness. The difference exists in exactly how these two conflicting aims are realized.

On Tory Island the participants make threats to establish just how tough they are, 'I'll surely do some killing tonight' and 'Hold me back or I'll kill him for sure.' To avoid the risk of actual fighting, they only make these threats if a crowd is present, ensuring that the protagonist can indeed be held back. The final solution is the production of a 'mother', and honour is maintained by claiming, 'I'd have had yer blood if me mother hadn't come.'

In the playground there are similar exchanges to establish toughness. For example, in Neill's long verbal battle with the girls, one child asserted, 'I'm not scared of you' and the other replied, 'I'm not scared of anybody.' Likewise, 'I could have broken your fingers' was answered with 'I could have broken yours as well.' But unlike on Tory Island, Neill did not use a ritual method for getting out of the conflict. His improvised solution was to 'fall asleep', so that an all out fight was avoided, and he was not seen to be ˜giving in. After all, as I said before, 'sleeping dogs do not have to answer bitches' taunts.'

On the football terraces actual fights, or rather harming the victim, are avoided by a mixture of the 'playground' and 'Tory Island' techniques. Sometimes fights are only picked if the police or older fans are nearby and able to intervene, while at other times the fans themselves announce, 'He's had enough', since only one or two blows at the most are required to settle even the most venomous face-to-face conflict.

Part of the football-terrace culture 'spills over' into the playground. At Middle School I saw twelve-year-old boys walk round chanting, 'Oxford aggro, Oxford aggro', and then picking 'fights' with the younger boys. But these fights were much more of the ritual 'aggro' type with only one or two actual blows and much shoving. Although they looked violent to the dinner-ladies, no one got hurt and many of the younger boys told me they enjoyed these encounters. Indeed, they might afford an introduction to the football culture for these novices.

The ordered way in which fights proceed is one example of ritual. Another is the peace formulae of the playground - 'bagsee', 'crucems', 'mercy' and 'taxi'. So, too, are the elaborate ceremonies of adult life - the marriage ceremony or the State Opening of Parliament. What all these have in common is that they are systems of signs which convey other than overt messages; only members of the particular community in question fully understand their significance, and part of that significance is the strong social pressure, that individuals within the community feel, that they ought to follow the ritual.

Another situation that adults and children both face and both solve by ritual is being introduced to a newcomer. The ritual that they use is more or less the same, though the elements are differently ordered. Rom Harré has described how strangers are introduced in contemporary adult British society and compares this to a small amount of observation by Don Mixon in an Oxford School of how seven- to ten-year-old boys cope with a newcomer in their midst. The adult ritual involves numerous sequential phases, including name exchange, formula of mutual recognition ('How do you do?'), physical contact (handshake), determination of identity (by reference to some status hierarchy or by a trial of strength, such as elbow wrestling), and lastly the formula of incorporation ('I'm so glad you could join us').

Amongst the schoolboys the ritual could be divided into three phases, all of which took place at playtime. On going out into the playground for the first time, the new boy was treated as simply 'not there' by a complete failure to look at or touch him, and so acknowledge his presence. This is in sharp contrast to

the adult ritual where the initial phases draw attention specifically to the presence of another human being. In the next
phase, some 'trial of strength' was suggested. Mixon observed
a game of football, which clearly was designed to see how the
stranger would cope. With his skill established, now the newcomer was talked to, jostled, patted, pushed and nudged as
the boys made their way back into class.

WHAT DO GAMES TEACH?

Just as the rituals of the playground may be introducing children to the idea that many everyday problems can be solved by
verbal formulae, so their games may serve as an introduction
to the attitudes, values and sex-roles appropriate for adult
society. For instance, in my introductory chapter I mentioned
Rivka Eifermann's finding that the games of kibbutzim children
are more co-operative and egalitarian than are the games of
moshav children. Each reflects adult values. Life in a moshav
is indeed less communal and less equal than in a kibbutz, but
how do these values come to be present in the children's games?
Do parents encourage some activities and not others, or is the
selection of games and the way they are played much more in
the children's hands? Brian Sutton-Smith, a New Zealand
psychologist, who has spent over a quarter of a century
researching into games, believes the latter is the case. He suggests that the motivation for game playing comes from the presence in the player of certain types of anxieties and conflicts,
which come about because of the way children are brought up.
The games recreate these conflicts, but within the protection
of play. Children gain through playing them a greater competence and confidence that transfers to the real-life situations
that they are anxious about. In other words, learning the
specific skills of the game brings more general lessons that are
relevant outside of the playground.
    As an example, Sutton-Smith suggests that games such as
'tag' and 'hide and seek' represent the child's anxieties about
being independent, since a player can either run out into
dangerous open spaces, or decide to stay in a safe area. He
tested his ideas by comparing anthropological evidence about the
games played by children and adults in 111 societies to information about their child-rearing practices. Chasing games were
indeed found to be most common in those cultures which stress
the importance of training their children to be independent.
    His survey showed that games of physical skill are present
in all cultures, but only in some are there in addition games
of strategy or games of chance. Cultures with only games of
physical skill tend to reward their children for any sort of
achievement. Games of strategy occur most in cultures which
stress obedience and games of chance were common particularly
in those cultures which reward responsibility.

Sutton-Smith summarizes his findings as follows:

> In the child's game we find a distillation of human relation-
> ships, particularly those having to do with power. As models
> of power, games serve to prepare children for expected life
> experiences. They are models of ways of succeeding over
> others, by magical power (as in games of chance), by force
> (as in physical skill games), or by cleverness (as in games
> of strategy). We have speculated that in games children
> learn all those necessary arts of trickery, deception, harass-
> ment, divination, and foul play that their teachers won't
> teach them but are most important in successful human
> relationships in marriage, business and war.

What types of power relationships are the children at my
Oxford schools being prepared for? Unless we look briefly at
the socioeconomic structure of adult British society, it would be
impossible to determine which games are in accord with, confirm
or reinforce the established values, and conversely which con-
tradict and flout them. Western industrial societies are based
on a combination of voluntary co-operation, regulated competition, contracts, and a judicial system involving a respect for
laws which protect the rights of the weak and powerful alike.
Although many societies obviously fail to live up to this ideal,
they could not function unless these attitudes were formed in
its members.

The games that I observed in the Oxford playgrounds seem
to provide just the right experience for this development. The
most popular ones involved a central person who orders,
controls, or tries to capture the rest of the group; for example,
'tig', 'hide and seek', 'British bulldog', 'mother may I?',
'grandmother's footsteps', to name but a few. These are com-
petitions according to a set of rules and often the group has
some degree of power to fight back. Sometimes they co-operate
by banding together, sometimes they co-operate by freeing
companions who have been caught.

Many of the disputes that arise during games reflect a rational
concern that the game should be played fairly, in such a way
as to give all players an equal chance. For instance, a child who
stays by the safety of the railings in off-ground-tig will be told,
'It's not fair if you don't run out.' Sometimes the principle of
equality is enshrined in the rules; in 'grandmother's footsteps',
the arrival of a new player during the game means that they
all must start again at the wall so that no one will have an
advantage.

Most games have the possibility for making contracts. At their
most rudimentary level, the children may not even be fully
aware of having entered into an agreement. For example, eight-
year-old Ramesh frequently let himself be caught by the youngest child in the group, his five-year-old brother, Mukesh. This
was not simply a case of pure altruism. I later noticed that

whenever the group selected who should be 'it', using the dip 'racing car, racing car, number nine', the little one always looked to the number of fingers that his brother held up; should he be the one asked, 'How many gallons did he use?', Ramesh's advice either helped himself or it helped Mukesh and in this way both brothers frequently managed to avoid being counted out.

The idea that cultural differences in games are rooted in socioeconomic differences comes from Michael Maccoby and his team, who spent two years in a small Mexican farming village, participating in and observing, both the children's play and games, and the adults' lifestyles. They found that the average village child, like a child in an industrialized society, proceeds from dramatic play to central-person games and then to team sports. But, a closer analysis revealed that their central-person games differ significantly in content and that their team games are innovations played by only particular villagers.

In the boys' versions of 'tig' and 'hide and seek', for example, the central person has either no authority and is chased or has full permission to punish the others who must try to escape. The group becomes a mass whose tyrannical role in a game precludes any co-operation either to act together, or to regulate the level of co-operation or to discuss how the game should be played.

These games mirror the values of adult life. A feudal past and semi-feudal present (since Zapata's revolution this century), have led to a distrust and hostility against all institutionalized authorities. In games, authority is represented as dangerous and impulsive, a force that a boy must either escape from or imitate. Likewise, in adult life there is little co-operation and any individual initiative is seen as a threat to the status quo. For example, there is only so much land, all of it in use. An ingenious new idea can only mean one person's gain at the expense of the others. Although it is true that adolescents play co-operative sports, which have been introduced relatively recently, they play them in a way that differs from industrialized societies. The villagers showed far less division of labour, either in soccer or in basketball, and any co-operation that they had was without leaders, individual stars or complex rules.

Maccoby suggests that play and games may serve a dual function; they both express, as well as form, traits of the culture. They both liberate a child from repressed conflicts and help him or her to master traumas of helplessness, as well as teach new attitudes, values and skills.

TEACHING NEW GAMES

Given this dual role of games, it would seem unlikely that introducing new games into a culture would have much effect on changing attitudes. This is exactly what Maccoby's team found when they tried to teach village children a new game that was a cross between 'British bulldog' and 'roll over'. It involved co-operation between 'thieves' against the 'Jefe', or 'Chief of Police', who stood in the middle. The 'Jefe' called a 'thief' to run over to the first safe area, and being caught meant joining him or her in the middle. A successful run to the second base enabled the 'thief' to call over all the other 'thieves', while the 'Chief' and any helpers had to catch as many of them as possible. The aim of the experiment was to see whether a more co-operative attitude against authority in play might begin to assert itself in real life. No such changes were forthcoming and the results were far different from what had been expected.

First of all, it proved impossible to get the boys and girls to play together because the girls left when the male 'Jefe' refused to call any of their names. When the boys played the game alone, they failed to stick to the rules as taught, but modified them in different ways, each expressing their attitudes towards authority. First, the 'thieves' showed anger and violent rebellion against the 'Jefe'. When a name was called, more than one ran out, and should they be caught, they fought back with pieces of wood that had been used to mark the safe areas. Next, the 'thieves' reacted with patient submission. Instead of trying to escape, they wanted to be caught. In the final stage of play, the game took on the aspect of a typical central-person game. Those who ran across safely immediately joined the 'Jefe' and his 'ayudantes' (helpers) and the concept of leader was lost as the group solidified to persecute the outside.

When the girls played the game they too modified its rules and refused to continue playing as they had been taught, despite careful explanations of the rules. They decided that the object of the game should be to be chosen as an 'ayudante' by the 'Jefe'. When called, they stepped forward proudly in order to be caught and stand with the 'Chief'.

The ways the children distorted the game lends support to the idea that their play unconsciously expresses their attitudes towards authority. The conclusion must be that if new games are to be taken up by children, then they should not be radically different from the old ones. In addition, their effect in terms of reforming an individual's attitudes is likely to be limited, since these attitudes, in part at least, reflect the socioeconomic structure of the society.

GAMES AND SEX-ROLES IN THE PLAYGROUND

The boys and girls tended to keep apart in the Oxford playgrounds, but they did get together for some activities. No doubt they learn many lessons in common, but do the 'boys only' and 'girls only' games teach them anything unique? When we examine these games, as well as the manner in which they separately played games which both sexes knew, it is possible to see a preparation for adult sex-roles.

With boys there was an emphasis on physical strength, achievement, and competitiveness. For example, both sexes usually selected roles by dipping which, of course, allowed plenty of scope for manipulating the rhyme, but only the boys also chose 'it' by joining hands, forming a circle around a drain-cover and trying to force each other to put a foot onto the grille. Girls, on the other hand, were far less competitive. They played variations of games which allowed for greater equality between the various roles and in their songs and rhymes showed an interest in family life. Some examples from the girls' repertoire demonstrate these differences.

The competitive element of many of their games was frequently of less importance than other aspects of the game. The hopping itself provided a good deal of amusement in 'hop, hop, hop, to the golliwog's shop....' The Opies heard boys reciting more or less the same rhyme, but with them it occurred within the context of a 'cock-fight', in which each tried to knock the other over, whilst balancing on one leg. Similarly, in 'mother may I?', the enjoyment lay mainly in the dialogue and contorted movements. When First School girls played 'follow-the-leader', the leader never demanded that those behind her do anything that was in the slightest bit difficult.

There were some varieties of chasing games that only girls played and these allowed greater equality between the chaser and those chased. For example, it was up to 'Mrs Brown' to decide when she would start the chase, by owning up to a fiendish desire to put 'brownies' in her stew. In the same way, 'Jack' could decide who to compete against in 'Jack, Jack, may we cross the water?', by only selecting those wearing a particular colour of clothing to run across.

One final difference between the sexes was the almost total lack of any of the girls' skipping or hand clapping rhymes in the boys' repertoire. Many of these songs emphasize the stages of life and typically suggest that the girls should look forward to having true love 'under the bramble bushes down by the sea', leading inevitably to getting married and raising a family 'with a boy for you and a girl for me.' Moreover, what message might be imparted through singing about a little Dutch girl who marries the boy who stole her necklace for the sole reason that he gave it back again? This couple, naturally enough, end up having a baby, going to heaven and becoming angels.

These sex differences in terms of boys' competitiveness and girls' interest in family life are not nearly so marked at Nursery School. Perhaps they develop most during the years at Primary School. Older children do indeed teach the younger ones their values. Recall the episode that my friend, William Maxwell, witnessed of how a ten-year-old boy taught a group of five-year-olds that hurting each other in 'roll over' could be fun.

Lastly, it is worth looking at the close fit between sex differences in the games of Mexican village children and preparation for adult sex-roles. As I have already mentioned, boys'

central-person games involved either one individual being
chased by the group or the whole group chasing a lone runner.
Girls' central-person games, on the other hand, had greater
variety and included competition in the form of chants and verbal contests. Their content precisely reflects both the predica-
ment faced by adult women in that society as well as their
strategies to cope.

Most of the girls' games refer to the dangers of the male
world. This lies not in sex, per se, but in the loss of personal
integrity, the fear of being used, the extreme of which is
being eaten alive. Once the man has satisfied his impulses he
goes away, leaving the unprotected girl to die. The games are
verbal warnings not to trust romantic love. Maccoby comments
that 'in this society, in which the male often does exploit the
woman, treating her alternately as a sexual object and as a
mother figure who must feed and baby him, the symbolism of
girls approximates the truth.'

Girls also learn the strategies that they might as adults use
to protect themselves from male violence. First, she might seek
solidarity with other girls by finding such cutting phrases to
describe them that they would rather join her than wait for
even more devastating descriptions that would expose them to
yet more ridicule and mirth from the others. Mature women are
even more ferocious with this type of verbal attack. A second
strategy is for girls to identify with the authority. In the case
of the new game that Maccoby introduced, they all wanted to
be the 'Chief's' helpers, while in adult life this frequently means
identifying with the husband and obeying him, but just so long
as he remains strong. This last point is crucial, for women's
identification with her spouse remains only as long as he demonstrates superior force. Should he weaken then they do not
hesitate to take charge, and even in games, girls seek and
enjoy authority much more than do boys. They were the only
ones to say that they liked central-person games, precisely
because of the authority that was allowed to the central role.

The games of the Mexican village farming community provide
us with a way of looking at our own culture. In both settings
games are a part of preparing children for life as adults in a
society which demands behaviour appropriate to their sex and
participation, if not a belief in, a particular socioeconomic
system.

THE PLAYGROUND AS A PREPARATION FOR ADULTHOOD

So far in this chapter I have shown that the playground world
is created and maintained by processes that are essentially
similar to those by which adults create and sustain their worlds.
Some of these similarities are at a general level, in terms of
values, attitudes, sex-roles and rituals. Other similarities are
at a more specific level; individuals of all ages are skilled at

manipulating each other using words alone. Any differences
between the activities and strategies in disputes of children
in the Nursery, First and Middle School and adults reflect the
different problems and needs that each age group faces. The
different worlds do not teach lessons that are in conflict, but
rather they co-operate to teach the skills, attitudes, values,
and beliefs that are appropriate for life at the time and also
are a good preparation for later on.

It is impossible ever to prove that experience in the playground is vital for the development of those skills that are going
to allow a child to manage him or herself successfully in the
adult world. No one has studied children whose sole deprivation
has been playtime and a researcher who suggested keeping
half a class inside at break and lunchtime would be highly
unpopular with pupils and Education Authorities alike. Moreover, the playground is only one opportunity for peer interaction. Even if children were deprived of peer experience, they
might still be able to learn the social skills that they lacked
later on. My point is merely that it is likely to be easier for
them to learn these skills in the playground.

GROWING UP WITH LIMITED OPPORTUNITY FOR PEER CONTACT

In some communities children grow up with very few opportunities to meet and play with their contemporaries. What little
evidence there is about these children's development comes
from a study by Hollos and Cowan comparing seven- to nine-
year-olds from three Norwegian settings. Some of them came
from a town, others from a village and others from a dispersed
farming community in the Arctic tundra. These last ones
rarely left their own homesteads before school age (eight years),
except for important holidays and family occasions. Their
interactions were confined to the family and mainly to one or
two siblings.

The only difference in the farm children's mental development
was in terms of their ability to put themselves in someone else's
shoes. The tasks measured the extent to which they could
report what another person would see, how well they could
repeat a story to another person who had never heard it before,
and whether they could take the role of story-teller in a car-
toon picture sequence. The farm children scored lowest on all
these tasks.

The researchers concluded that a minimal level of interaction
with peers and adults is necessary for the adequate development of role-taking and that the children in the farming
community were below it. It may well be, however, that life as
adults in these isolated communities involves far simpler social
situations which do not demand to the same extent the ability
to see someone else's perspective.

THE DEVELOPMENT OF SOCIAL SENSITIVITY

Some ability to put oneself into another person's shoes is vital for the development of the social skills that I have described in this book. Knowing another person's goals and how they will interpret your actions underlies all the strategies that I have discussed. A certain amount of peer interaction may be the minimal requirement for the development of social sensitivity, but over and above that, the type of interaction with parents is crucial.

Paul Light has shown, in a recent study in Cambridge, that mothers who are more sensitive in the way they treat their four-year-olds have children who are themselves more aware of other people's viewpoints and are judged by their infant school teachers at five to be better socially adjusted. The 'sensitive' mothers said they avoided interfering in their children's quarrels ('usually if I can stand it, it wears itself out'), gave emotional support when their children had temper tantrums ('feeling embarrassed is often the cause, I have to really cuddle and comfort him') and conceded to the children's wishes when they failed to respond to requests ('well if it's not too vital and she thinks she's busy, I let her get on with it'). Less sensitive mothers more often smacked their children in these situations. Surprisingly perhaps, these attitudes were not at all associated with any differences in social class.

The characteristics that distinguish sensitive and less sensitive mothers is their capacity to consider the child as if he or she were an equal, despite the obvious inequalities of their relationship. Light quotes two different reactions of mothers, should their youngsters fail to comply with a request, because they are engrossed in play. First the mother of the least socially sensitive child in the group:

I usually say you'll do it now, I've told you to do it. I don't like the way some people perhaps say 'will you do this for me' and then don't insist.

By way of contrast, the mother of the child with the highest score of Light's various sensitivity tasks:

Yes, perhaps she'll not do it straight away, but then I'm like that. If I'm busy doing something I'll say 'well wait a minute' - so it works both ways I suppose.

We can see how the socially sensitive mothers may have their effect if we examine the development of ritual. John and Elizabeth Newson report that rituals are performed at bedtime by about one in three pairs of mothers and their offspring from their sample of 700 children growing up in Nottingham. The ritual need not be elaborate. 'It may simply be that the final kiss is given in an exact and special manner: the mother is

obliged to "kiss me first, then teddy, then me on the nose",
or to "give a kiss for each finger and a great big hug".' The
most frequent type of ritual is the verbal one, 'in particular,
it tends to be the words of parting which take the form of a
recognized incantation.' If the ritual is not performed, or the
traditional formula is varied, then the child 'will typically
refuse to settle down at all until the phrases have been correctly
recited.'
    The Newsons suggest that:

> bearing in mind that bedtime is not the only context in which
> ritualistic behaviour may occur (though it is almost certainly
> the major opportunity for this), we may conclude that such
> behaviour is sufficiently commonplace to be regarded as a
> normal manifestation of this stage of development.

Like Paul Light, they found no indications of a sex or class
bias, though children from the lowest socioeconomic class
(class v) showed significantly less ritual. These families were
in general more casual with regard to bedtime.
    Why do so many four-year-olds indulge in these rituals at
bedtime? The fact that they are so commonplace suggests to the
Newsons that they cannot just be explained in terms of the
children's need for security.

> That so many rituals ever become established reflects some-
> thing more: that the parents of these children are, on the
> whole, extremely tolerant of such demands and are in general
> prepared to involve themselves rather deeply in what might
> be considered childish whims and fancies. No doubt there is
> some element of expediency in their indulgence - most parents
> know from experience that it can take a very long while for
> an angry and frustrated child to fall asleep - but, over and
> above this, parents seem to believe, and to behave as if,
> their children have a right to be humoured in this way; they
> will take on trust the child's own evaluation of his behaviour
> as necessary and justifiable.

It may well be that parents who are sensitive in this way unwittingly give their children an advantage when it comes to learning
ritual words like 'bagsee' a few years hence. The child who
uses it has mastered a far more socially sensitive solution than
just grabbing.

GROWING UP IN THE PLAYGROUND

In this book I have described how children interact with one
another when they are more or less free from adult supervision.
Much of my material concerns games and the conflicts that can
arise during them. By thinking about what the children say at

such times, I have been able to uncover the implicit and explicit
knowledge that is shared by members of the playground community, and this knowledge is extensive. Children know enormous numbers of games and songs. For those individuals who
have difficulty in remembering anything at all in class, this may
seem a remarkable feat, but they have much greater motivation
to learn the lessons of the playground, for this knowledge
brings more immediate rewards. They learn how to join in a
game, how to choose and avoid roles, how to deal with people
who cheat or make trouble, and above all else how to manipulate
situations to their own advantage.

\ All in all, what the playground offers is an enormous scope to
initiate, discuss, influence and change rules in a way that we
cannot imagine happening between children and adults.\ Indeed,
when teachers supervise play it is exactly these types of
opportunities that are missing. Sylvia Knopp Polgar watched
the way teachers organize games in United States Elementary
Schools. She found that they insisted on order, allowed the
children little flexibility in following the rules, randomly
assigned them to groups rather than let them decide for themselves and set the same expectations for all of them. Even when
adults try to fit in with children's interest, they can never be
an equal in the way that another child can. Although it is
impossible to prove, all the evidence points to the vital importance of peer interaction, even though its message is not
fundamentally different from that which comes from adults. Both
influences play an important role in the process of social development.

The playground, and free-play in the Nursery, are both very
important contexts in which to begin to appreciate that doing
things together can be fun and children are eager to find a way
in which they can co-operate. Whilst many succeed, there are
some who find this adjustment more difficult. They tend to get
themselves repeatedly into almost identical situations in which
they always react in the same way. These children do not
experiment like 'normal' children in new games, new roles, new
situations and new ways out of difficulties. They are, so to
speak, 'in a rut' and it is this limited quality of 'difficult'
children's behaviour which gives most cause for concern. It
suggests that these children are constrained by their expectations of hostility from others and they they are unlikely to
modify their behaviour of their own accord unless their expectations can be dispelled. In fact, because other children tend to
reject their teasing, boasting and displaying approaches, their
expectations are fulfilled and their behaviour continues. It is
these difficult children that Margaret Manning and I are watching
in their last year at four Edinburgh Nursery Schools. We hope
to better understand 'what makes them tick' and suggest ways
in which the teachers might intervene to help them overcome
their difficulties. Moreover, teachers at Nursery School are in a
much better position to intervene than their colleagues at

Primary School, where classes are much more formally organized.
It is not simply a matter of 'catching them young'.

Of the many aspects of playground life that I would like to
study further, cheating at choosing 'it' comes top of the list.
I have never ceased to be impressed by the speed and accuracy
of children's mental arithmetic as they count ahead when asked
to say a number in participation dips such as 'Racing car
number nine'. Even children with an exceedingly poor grasp
of spoken English not only participated in this group activity,
but succeeded in manipulating others at such times. I doubt
whether these children in particular would show the same
arithmetic skills, when asked by a teacher to perform essentially the same task, but outside the context of the game. Even
more interesting is that the mathematical concept of a random
number arises in the game from a social motivation: the need
to be fair. The game introduces children to a mathematical
concept that they are not taught formally until much later.

I hope that observing the playground world would lead
teachers to share my conclusions. First, that children are learning all sorts of social skills and second, that in the activities
of their own choice, many children are much more sophisticated
than could be guessed from their classroom performance.

When I first started watching at playtime I asked a Head
Teacher and five-year-old Jon what there is to learn in the
playground. The Head Teacher told me that anything a child
learns in the playground could equally well be learnt in the
classroom and she looked forward 'to the day when noisy play-
times were considered a thing of the past.' Indeed, this has
already happened in some schools which favour modern 'child-
centered' teaching methods. The children are presumed to
enjoy their new found freedom in lessons to such an extent that
they have no need for a break. Five-year-old Jon's comment
was quite the reverse. He told me quite simply that playtime
'makes me grow up extremely slowly.' It is to him that this book
is dedicated.

Notes

CHAPTER 1: 'WHAT DO YOU THINK PLAYTIME'S FOR?'

In recent years there has been much criticism of the experimental approach in social and developmental psychology. For instance, Urie Bronfenbrenner (1977) notes that most studies of child development have pursued 'rigour' at the expense of 'relevance' and this emphasis has led to a massive preponderance of experimental rather than observational studies. He laments that although these experiments may have been elegantly designed they are often limited in scope. They involve situations that are unfamiliar, artificial, and short-lived and call for unusual behaviours that are difficult to generalize to other settings. Bronfenbrenner characterizes contemporary child psychology as 'the science of the strange behaviour of children in strange situations with strange adults for the briefest possible periods of time.'
Peter Warr (1973, 1977) has made similar criticisms of other branches of psychology. He suggests that the preference for 'rigour' has arisen, because most research problems are derived from entirely within the literature of the discipline, rather than from the 'real' world outside the laboratory.
But developmental psychology has not always been like this and of late there have been welcome signs of change. During the 1920s and 1930s there was a great deal of observational work on preschool children, conducted mostly in the United States. However, Smith and Connolly (1972) were disappointed to find that the current generation of researchers almost totally neglect this extensive literature on physical, intellectual and social development, and behaviour problems. For thirty years naturalistic observation was eclipsed by behaviourism, but the tradition re-emerged in the late 1960s under the title of human ethology.
Human ethology is based on the successes of animal ethology. Niko Tinbergen, who himself moved from studying animals to people, describes it quite simply as 'watching and wondering.' But human ethologists watch and wonder in a much more rigorous way than the earlier researchers of preschool children. They stress the need for systematic observation of behaviour, using categories which are often defined at a basic level, coupled with techniques of analysis to find out which behaviours follow each other and in what contexts they occur. They are also concerned to explain behaviour within an evolutionary framework, continually asking about the advantage that it might bring to the individual. Despite these characteristics, reviews of the discipline by Blurton-Jones (1972), Smith (1974) and Bateson and Hinde (1976) reveal how widely its scope has been interpreted. Nevertheless, nearly all of the work reported so far has concerned the interactions of three- to five-year-olds or what mothers and their babies do together.
What about the interactions of children younger than preschool age? Lewis and Rosenblum (1975) report the first work in this area. As for observations of what children older than five do outside the classroom, whether in street or playground, the few studies that have been completed are discussed in the present volume.
The ethological observations of playtime reflect the characteristics that I have already mentioned. Don Omark (1980) watched in Swiss, Ethiopian and United States playgrounds in order to understand how the perception of dominance relations might be adaptive for the individual. He believes it has

importance beyond reducing potential conflict, since in order to perceive a
dominance hierarchy, children must learn the more general skill of how to
infer a series from only limited information, in this case from observations of
encounters between only a few children at a time (see also Sluckin and Smith,
1977). Dan Freedman's (1974) extensive notes on the play of five- to seven-
year-olds in playgrounds in cultures in many parts of the world stemmed from
an interest in the biological basis of sex differences.

Rivka Eifermann called her work ethological because it involved highly
systematic observation. Her view of games as an indicator of the nature of
the adult culture reflects a theme that runs through much of the writings
about play (see Avedon and Sutton-Smith, 1971 and Margaret Mead, 1975).
The most interesting collection of original papers on this whole area is edited
by Bruner, Jolly and Sylva (1976) and is organized around four topics: the
evolutionary context, play and the world of objects and tools, play and the
social world, and play and the world of symbols.

Jean Piaget's study of marbles charts the child's developing awareness of
just one aspect of his social environment. But although we normally think of
Piaget as having been influenced by biology, his participant observation in
games of marbles, so as to understand the child's own perspective, has
parallels to anthropology. This attempt to gain insight into the social world of
the child through observation and interview was not taken up again for many
years. When studies did begin to appear, the new emphasis had changed
mainly to asking children about their understanding of social matters such
as justice, friendship, authority rules, manners and sex-role conventions,
rather than observing how they use this knowledge in everyday interaction
(see review by Damon, 1977).

Something similar to Piaget's approach has been advocated in Harré and
Secord's (1972) important critique of experimental social psychology, entitled
'The Explanation of Social Behaviour' (see also Harré 1977a, 1977b, 1979).
They believe that an adequate science of people should 'treat them as if they
were human beings' and this means taking seriously what they say. Like the
ethologists they want 'to study human lives as they are really lived, not in
the strange and impoverished world of laboratories, but out in the streets, at
home, in shops and cafes and lecture rooms where people really interact.' But
their science of ethogeny goes way beyond ethology, since they recommend
talking to the people whose actions are being studied. The only animal
ethologist to have had this opportunity was the celebrated Dr Dolittle. Analysis of the explanations that are given for action or accounts, as the etho-
genists call them, is one way of finding out how an individual makes sense of
the social world. The other method is to examine naturally occurring speech
and in particular language that is used towards some goal in social interaction.

Iona and Peter Opie provide this second type of material in their book
'The Lore and Language of Schoolchildren'. When Rom Harré read it, he
wondered whether the methods of social management in the playground are
similar to those of adult life (1974, 1975), and if so, just how important might
such experience be? To find out, he suggested further microsociology, like
that of the Opies where adult perceptions were brought to bear on playground
life, as well as the collection and analysis of spontaneously produced speech
to understand the children's own theories of their social world. In order to
discover the continuities in social management techniques, we would also need
to know much more about the precise nature of the various adult social worlds.

Although ethology and ethogeny appear to be quite different approaches
to the study of human lives, they are not incompatible. Ethology emphasizes
non-participant observation and a biological framework of explanation, while
ethogeny uses participant observation and favours cultural explanations, but
a strict dichotomy between the two is misleading. I have argued elsewhere
(Smith and Sluckin, 1979) that the greatest progress is likely to be made
by combining the two approaches.

CHAPTER 2: 'HEY MISTER, CAN I BE IN YOUR BOOK?'

An ethologist does not interact with the individuals that are being watched, since he or she does not want to have any effect on their behaviour. Though there has been research to show that preschool children will more often approach an observer who talks or smiles rather than ignore them, such a silence seemed to have just the opposite effect with the older children, and particularly those at Middle School. The important point concerning validity in my study is not that at times I talked to the children, but that they did not see me as an authority figure and continued to sort out conflicts in their own way despite my close proximity. Of course, I tried to be as 'invisible' as possible and rather than face them often stood sideways on and avoided eye contact, whilst recording into my dictaphone exactly what was being said.

Not only should a study be valid and come to conclusions that are clearly supported by the data, but it should also be reliable. We are entitled to ask whether the same observer if he or she observed at a different time, or indeed a new observer, would come to the same conclusions. When I attempted to find out 'who did what with whom' at playtime by watching each child for three minute periods, I randomly moved between children so as to gain an idea of the whole range of activities. After each thirty-second interval within the three-minute periods, I scored the predominant activity according to a list of well-defined categories. But how consistent was I and how easily communicable would these definitions be to another researcher? To find out I followed the advice of Smith and Connolly (1972) in assessing both these aspects of reliability through comparing my own scoring to that of another trained observer during a single hour-long play session. We achieved 90 per cent agreement as to whether a child was solitary or interacting, 80 per cent as to the number of companions (if interacting) and 60 per cent as to what the child was doing. However, these figures would vary according to the amount of training and the cultural background of the observer and in any case, the level of acceptable inter-observer agreement can only be arbitrarily set.

Ethogenic researchers are also concerned with collecting data in a reliable way and coming to valid conclusions, but they do not share the ethologists' belief that such characteristics of a study can be easily quantified. But of course they are careful to describe exactly how they proceed, in terms of what episodes they watch for and how the data is analysed, so that any study could be repeated by researchers in other settings. Also, the goal of the ethogenic enterprise is quite different to that of the ethologists. They aim to understand the perspective of the individuals being studied and do so through a process of negotiation testing with the individuals concerned any interpretations as to how they see their world. Just like anthropologists, a thorough and continual process of negotiation between researcher and participant is held to ensure reliability and validity (see Marsh, Rosser and Harré, 1978).

A thorough review of research findings on sex differences has been compiled by Maccoby (1966), but for more recent United States findings on differences in social behaviour see Dweck and Bush (1976). Hartup (1978) discusses mixed age playgroups in a review called 'children and their friends'. The most up-to-date guide to the way schools are approaching education for a multi-racial society is a report compiled for the schools council by researchers from The National Foundation for Educational Research (NFER) and The National Association for Multi-Racial Education (NAME) 'Multi-Racial Education: Curriculum and Content 5 to 13'.

CHAPTER 4: 'BAGSEE NO BAGSEES'

In this chapter I have tried to reveal some order in the way children solve social problems. It turned out that they use particular strategies and that these rest upon the knowledge that children have about other individuals and social interaction. In other words, my aim is not simply to list the children's tactics, but to go further and explore the abilities that underlie the creation and maintenance of an orderly playground community.

The empirical data quoted in chapter 3 onward are of my own descriptions, whispered into a portable dictaphone, of what children did and said to produce solutions to problems they met. These descriptions were collected, both whilst watching each child's activities in turn at First and Middle School, and also from a period of two months at First School when I scanned the playground for problems. Initially my criteria for what to record as a problem were relatively loose; a dispute was defined as 'any clash of wills or argument between children'. Later on I became more specific as to the types of episodes that I wanted to look out for; the occurrence of fights, threats, racist comments, arguments, teasing, nicknaming, actions of gangs, bullying, problems of ownership, bargaining, methods of choosing roles and the problems presented to the playground supervisors. I was not just watching for aggressive behaviour in the playground, but rather for situations that if not managed skilfully could lead to this type of outcome. Since by and large the children solved problems by words alone, my study reveals some of the ways in which children can avoid violence at playtime.

The analysis of the episodes involved a number of concepts from Rom Harré's ethogenic approach to social psychology. The most important is the distinction between what we intend our actions to mean and how others interpret them, and some interpretations seem more reasonable than others, because we make sense of an action within the context of what is going on already.

These distinctions are important because the extent to which social action can be clearly interpreted delineates a dimension of solutions. At one extreme, the meaning of the action is clear while at the other, the meaning is open to a number of conflicting interpretations. Ritual words such as 'bagsee', 'crucems', 'taxi' and 'mercy' have clear meanings and are rarely challenged. Similarly, some situations have rules that everyone knows about and it is usually clear when they are being followed. In chapter 4 I discuss joining in a game in this light.

I have called verbal ritual and following the rules standard solutions because they rely on conventional meanings. Other solutions involve alternative interpretations and do so in a variety of ways. A child may feel it is necessary to restate the definition of the situation (e.g. 'We're playing "tig" not "bulldog"') or a number of children might agree as to the nature of the situation but argue about the implications for what is allowed (e.g. discuss the rules of hopscotch). Both these solutions seem to clarify the way ambiguous actions should be interpreted and do so by making the context clear.

Some solutions are more drastic and children deliberately attempt to change the interpretation of an action to gain some advantage. One way of changing the interpretation is to inform another child of the unfortunate future consequences of his or her actions, should they occur. If Johnny knows what Jimmy values at playtime, then this strategy can be successful (e.g. 'I'll not be your friend if you don't give me a sweet'). In chapter 7 I examine children's various goals in the playground. As for re-interpreting actions that have already occurred, I have identified essentially three different techniques; the meaning of the action can be changed by either redefining the nature of the situation, or by redefining the individual responsible, or by redefining what has happened.

If the new definition of the situation automatically discounts the action, then this can be called situational discounting (e.g. after a punch has been thrown a child may claim, 'It's only a game, I didn't mean it really'). Redefining the individual could involve denying agency (e.g. 'It wasn't me'), or somehow discounting the person as not properly responsible for his or her own actions (e.g. 'He's ill'). Lastly, redefining what has happened might involve a denial that it happened at all (e.g. 'You didn't tig me'), or a relabelling of the action so as to place it in a better or worse light (e.g. 'You let him go' becomes 'He forced his way out'), or a change in the moral tone that we normally associate with the act (e.g. after making a mistake, a child claims, 'You can't always be right, can you').

The point about the framework that I have outlined is not that it provides clear-cut categories for observation, but rather that it gives us some clues as to how to understand the way children manipulate each other with words. It is very much a first attempt to state some of the features that a theory ought to be concerned with, namely distinguishing between the intention and interpretation of action, between standard and alternative interpretations, between verbal ritual, following the rules, clarifying and changing the meaning and between redefining the situation, the individual and the act. These concepts are implicit in the way I analyse the episodes of conflicts throughout the book.

Bibliography

Avedon, E.M., and Sutton-Smith, B. (1971), 'The Study of Games',
New York: Wiley.
Barker, R.G., and Wright, H.F. (1955), 'Midwest and its Children',
New York: Harper & Row.
Bateson, P.G.C., and Hinde, R.A. (1976), 'Growing points in ethology',
Cambridge: Cambridge University Press.
Blurton-Jones, N.G. (1972), 'Ethnological Studies of Child Behaviour',
Cambridge: Cambridge University Press.
Boyle, Jimmy (1977), 'A Sense of Freedom', Edinburgh: Canongate Press.
Briggs, R. (1977), 'Fungus the Bogeyman', London: Hamish Hamilton.
Bronfenbrenner, U. (1977), Towards an Experimental Ecology of Human
Development', 'American Psychologist', 32, 7, 513-31.
Bruner, J.S., Jolly, A., and Sylva, K. (1976), 'Play - its role in development
and evolution', Harmondsworth: Penguin.
Damon, W. (1977), 'The Social World of the Child', San Francisco: Jossey-Bass.
Dawe, H.L. (1934), An analysis of two hundred quarrels of preschool children,
'Child Development', 5, 139-57.
Dweck, C.S. and Bush, E.S. (1976), Sex differences in learned helplessness:
I. Differential debilitation with peer and adult evaluators, 'Developmental
Psychology', 12, 147-56.
Eifermann, R., (1970), Co-operativeness and egalitarianism in kibbutz
children's games, 'Human Relations', 23, 6, 579-87.
Farb, P. (1977), 'Word Play', London: Coronet.
Fox, R. (1977), The Inherent Rules of Fighting, in Collett, P. (ed.),
'Social Rules and Social Behaviour', Oxford: Basil Blackwell.
Freedman, D.G. (1974), 'Human Infancy: an evolutionary perspective',
New York: Wiley.
Goldstein, K. (1971), Strategy in counting out: an ethnographic folklore
field study, in E.M. Avedon and B. Sutton-Smith (eds), 'The Study of
Games', New York: Wiley.
Hargreaves, D.H. (1967), 'Social Relations in a Secondary School',
London: Routledge & Kegan Paul.
Harré, R. (1974), The conditions for a social psychology of childhood in
MPM Richards (ed.), 'The Integration of a Child Into a Social World',
Cambridge: Cambridge University Press.
— (1975), The origins of social competence in a pluralist society, 'Oxford
Review of Education', 1, 151-8.
— (1977a), The ethogenic approach: theory and practice, in L. Berkowitz
(ed.), 'Advances in Experimental Psychology', vol.10, London: Academic
Press.
— (1977b), Automatisms and autonomies: in reply to Professor Schlenker, in
L. Berkowitz (ed.), 'Advances in Experimental Psychology', vol.10,
London: Academic Press.
— (1979), 'Social Being', Oxford: Basil Blackwell.
Harré, R., and DeWaele, J.P. (1976), The ritual for incorporation of a
stranger, in R. Harré (ed.), 'Life Sentences', London: Wiley.
Harré, R., and Secord, P.F. (1972), 'The Explanation of Social Behaviour',
Oxford: Basil Blackwell.
Hartup, W. (1978), Children and their friends, in H. McGurk (ed.),

'Issues in Childhood Social Development', London: Methuen.
Hollos, M., and Cowan, P.A. (1973), Social isolation and cognitive develop-
ment. Logical operations and role-taking abilities in three Norwegian settings,
'Child Development', 44, 630-41.
Lee, Laurie (1959), 'Cider with Rosie', London: Hogarth Press.
Lewis, M., and Rosenblum, L.A. (1975), 'Friendship and Peer Relations',
London: Academic Press.
Light, P. (1979), 'The Development of Social Sensitivity', Cambridge:
Cambridge University Press.
Maccoby, E. (1966), Classified summary of research in sex difference, in
E. Maccoby (ed.), 'The Development of Sex Differences', Stanford:
Stanford University Press.
Maccoby, M., Modiano, N., Lander, P. (1964), Games and social character
in a Mexican village, 'Psychiatry', 27, 150-62; reprinted in B. Sutton-Smith
(ed.) (1973).
Manning, M., Heron, J., and Marshall, T. (1978), Styles of hostility and
social interactions at nursery, at school and at home. An extended study
of children, in L.A. Hersov, M. Berger, and D. Shaffer (eds), 'Aggression
and Anti-Social Behaviour in Childhood and Adolescence', Monograph of
the Journal of Child Psychology and Psychiatry, vol.1, Oxford: Pergamon
Press.
Marsh, P., Rosser, E., and Harré, R. (1978), 'The Rules of Disorder',
London: Routledge & Kegan Paul.
Mead, M. (1943), 'Coming of Age in Samoa', Harmondsworth: Penguin.
First published, 1928.
— (1975), Children's Play Style: Potentialities and Limitations of its Use as
a Cultural Indicator, 'Anthropological Quarterly', 48, 157-82.
Montagner, H. (1978), 'L'enfant et la Communication', Paris: Pernoud/Stock.
Morris, D., Collett, P., Marsh, P., and O'Shaugnessy, M. (1979),
'Gestures: their origin and distribution', London: Cape.
Neill, S.R. St.J. (1976), Aggression in pre-adolescent boys, 'Journal of
Child Psychology and Psychiatry', 17, 213-20.
Newson, J., and Newson, E. (1968), 'Four Years Old in an Urban Community',
London: Allen & Unwin.
Omark, D.R., Freedman, D.G., and Strayer, F. (1980), 'Dominance
Relations: Ethological Perspectives on Human Conflict', New York: Garland.
Opie, I., and Opie, P. (1959), 'The Lore and Language of School Children',
London and New York: Oxford University Press.
— (1969), 'Children's Games in Street and Playground', London and New York:
Oxford University Press.
Piaget, J. (1932), 'The Moral Judgment of the Child', London: Routledge
& Kegan Paul.
Polgar, S.K. (1976), The social context of games: or when is play not play,
'Sociology of Education', 49, 265-71.
Rushforth, Winifred (1981), 'Something is Happening: Spiritual Awareness
and Psychology in the New Age', London: Turnstone Books.
Sluckin, A.M., and Smith, P.K. (1977), Two approaches to the concept of
dominance in preschool children, 'Child Development', 48, 917-23.
Smith, P.K. (1974), Ethological methods, in B.M. Foss (ed.), 'New
Perspectives in Child Development', Harmondsworth: Penguin.
Smith, P.K., and Connolly, K. (1972), Patterns of play and social interaction
in preschool children, in N. Blurton Jones (ed.), 'Ethological Studies of
Child Behaviour', Cambridge: Cambridge University Press.
Smith, P.K., and Sluckin, A.M. (1979), Ethology, ethogeny, etics, emics,
biology, culture: on the limitations of dichotomies, 'European Journal of
Social Psychology', 9, 397-415.
Sutton-Smith, B. (1973), 'Child Psychology', New York: Appleton-Century-
Crofts, 356-7.
Sutton-Smith, B. (ed.) (1973), 'Readings in Child Psychology', New York:
Appleton-Century-Crofts.
Thompson, F. (1973), 'Lark Rise to Candleford', Harmondsworth: Penguin.

Tinbergen, N. (1969), Ethology, in R. Harré (ed.), 'Scientific thought 1900-1960: a selective survey', Oxford: Oxford University Press.
— (1975), The importance of being playful, 'The Times Educational Supplement', 10 January.
Turner, I., Factor, J., and Lowenstein, L. (1978), 'Cinderella Dressed in Yella': Heinemann Educational.
Umaoka, K. (1974), The social function of Janken play in Japanese preschool children, '(The Japanese) Journal of Child Development', 10, 17-28.
Warr, P. (1973), Towards a more human psychology, 'Bulletin of the British Psychological Society', 26, 1-8.
— (1977), Aided Experiments in social psychology, 'Bulletin of the British Psychology Society', 30, 2-8.
Zivin, G. (1977), On becoming subtle: age and social rank changes in the use of a facial gesture, 'Child Development', 48, 1314-21.

Index

'French touch', 20
Freud, Sigmund, 4
friendship, 11, 45-6, 48, 59, 62-4
'Fungus the Bogeyman', 19

games - aggression specialists, 81
games: lessons of, 110-12; power
  relationships and values, 110-12
goals at playtime, 61-75
Goldstein, Kenneth, 17
'Good morning Mrs Brown...', 20, 114
'grandmother's footsteps', 22
guessing games, 25-6

'hammer and nails', 18
hand clapping games, 26-9, 114
harassment aggression, 80-1
Hargreaves, David, 97
Harré, Rom, 109-10, 126, 127
'hide and seek', 21
Hollos, M., 116-17
'Hop, hop, hop to the butcher's
  shop...', 18
'Hop, hop, hop to the golliwog's
  shop...', 17-18
'hopping tig', 19
hopscotch, 26
'hospital tig', 19
'Humpty Dumpty sat on a wall...', 30

'I draw a snake upon your back...',
  21
'I hold my little finger...', 21
'I'm the little Dutch girl, Dutch girl,
  Dutch girl...', 29
insults, 74-5, 102-12
interaction styles, 76-81
introduction rituals, 109-10
'ip, dip...', 14
'I went to a Chinese restaurant...', 13

'Jack, Jack, may we cross the water?',
  20
'James Hunt races', 21
'Janken play', 107-8
'jets', 32, 103
joining in a game, 45-6, 56, 62

kibbutzim games, 3-4, 110
'kiss chase', 20, 70, 102

'Last onto the wall is "it"', 17, 51
leaders, 77-81
'leapfrog', 24
learning in the playground, 1-2, 26,
  29, 98-120
Lee, Laurie, 104
Light, Paul, 117-18
'line tig', 19
'lolly sticks', 23
'loo tig', 19

Maccoby, Michael, 112-13, 114-15
'Make friends, make friends...', 63
Manning, Margaret, 76-81, 96, 106,
  119
marbles, 4, 26, 33
Marsh, Peter, 108-9
Mead, Margaret, 4
'mercy', 24, 38-9, 44, 59, 103
'mercy touch', 24
Middle School, transition to, 11
'Miss Mary Black, Black, Black...',
  27
mixed-age groups, 9-11
Mixon, Don, 109-10
Montagner, Hubert, 76-81, 96, 106
moral judgment, 4
Morris, Desmond, 104-5
moshav games, 3-4, 110
'mother may I?', 22

Neill, Sean, 40
new games, 112-13
Newson, John and Elizabeth, 117-18
nicknames and epithets, 55-6, 60, 65-
  9, 101

observational methods, 2-3
observations: details of method, 8-9;
  reliability and validity of, 123
'off-ground-tig', 78
'Oh Susie was a baby...', 28
Opie, Iona and Peter, 2, 14-26, 31-2,
  63, 107, 114
owning a game, 47-8
'Oxford and Cambridge', 23

'paper, scissors, stone', 107-8
participation dips, 16-17
peer contact, 98, 116-17
Piaget, Jean, 4, 35, 105, 106
'piggyback fights', 23
'piggyback tig', 19
Plato, 4
playing with words, intention and
  interpretation, 35-44, 59, 99-101
'plus' face, 101-2
Polgar, Sylvia Knopp, 119
'policemen', 22
'polo', 23
'postman's knock', 25, 69
precedence, 37
problems at playtime, 45-60

'queenie', 25-6

'Ra, ra, chuckeree, chuckeree...', 16
racial minority children, 11-12, 47,
  67-9
'Racing car, racing car, number
  nine...', 16, 52
racing games, 22-3, 71-3, 83-4, 91